# Bill's Basics

# Bill's Basics

Bill Granger

Quadrille
PUBLISHING

# Contents

## A few words

The chances are, if you're reading this, you own a few cookbooks already. Some of them probably fall open at dog-eared pages featuring the favourite recipes you cook time and time again. These much-loved 'basics' are your regular lifesavers because they're simple to make, turn out right every time and taste delicious.

For *Bill's Basics* I wanted to create a one-stop manual of my personal favourites. This is my own repertoire of simple classics that should keep you covered for every occasion from lazy breakfast to healthy lunch, quick snack, intimate dinner or late-night supper for a crowd. It does me.

These dishes draw on all my fondest food memories, and most have their roots planted in the past, near and far, which brings about a strong sense of nostalgia when I'm cooking. However, I don't have time to be too nostalgic — I've still got to get dinner on the table. And I don't stand on ceremony, so most of these classics have been spruced up and given a little kick or twist from the original to bring them deliciously and simply into the third millennium.

Trends come and go, and our attitudes to food — buying it, cooking it and eating it — have changed radically over the last couple of decades, but certain classics have stood the test of time. The only thing I found difficult when writing this book was keeping my selection down to 100 recipes. Not including some dishes felt like saying goodbye to old friends.

Over the years I've found that the simplest recipes often get the most positive feedback. And my basics certainly aren't about elaborate cooking. If you love the flavours of coq au vin or Thai beef salad, but have always imagined them tricky to cook at home, please give my basic versions a try. A lot of my cooking is about taking a few clever short cuts and being happy in the knowledge that you've saved time and energy but haven't skimped on great taste. (And a well-justified pride that you haven't resorted to takeaways or processed ready meals!)

My only real rule in the kitchen is to taste whatever you're cooking as often as you can. Everyone's tastes vary (mine change all the time), and your idea of a pinch of salt or squeeze of lemon might be different from the next cook's. So, please, have fun and enjoy the time spent preparing and eating simple, classic, good food with family and friends. There really is nothing better.

People often ask if I ever get tired of making breakfast, as it's the meal for which I'm best known. The answer is no. It's just the best way to start the day — and if something that's doing you so much good can also feel like an indulgence, I think that's marvellous.

While a lot of us are enthusiastic about new flavours and exotic ingredients for dinner, we're often less adventurous in the morning. We prefer something familiar to help us face the day. For that reason, I think, breakfast basics never really change, but we can always find inspiration by looking to different cultures.

The world contains many delicious variations on egg breakfasts: pancakes, kedgeree, eggs Benedict and, a new favourite of mine, shakshouka, a sort of Israeli fry-up. Porridge is quintessentially Scottish, hash browns as American as apple pie, and French toast… well, was it first made in France, I wonder?

# Breakfast

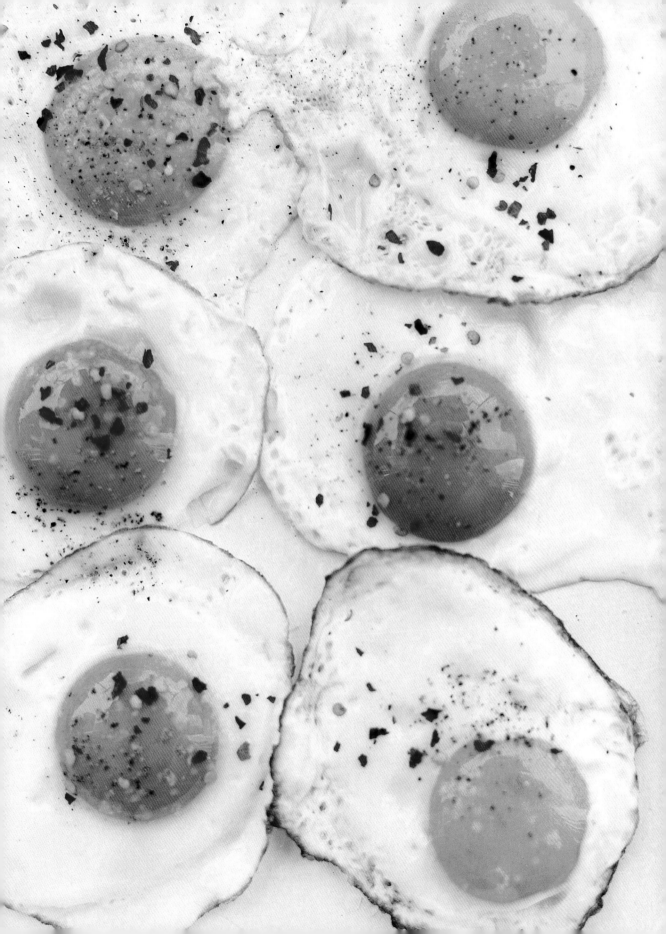

# Pancakes

I could've written an entire book of pancake recipes. I finally narrowed it down to one recipe I really love, probably because it's the quickest and easiest. Buttermilk pancakes are a great classic, but buttermilk is usually a special purchase in my house. I never seem to have it when the family are demanding pancakes on a Sunday. Use buttermilk if you have it, but adding lemon juice to the milk will create a substitute – so that you don't have to go to the shops in your pyjamas.

2 tablespoons lemon juice
300ml milk
200g plain flour
3 teaspoons baking powder
2 tablespoons caster sugar
2 eggs, lightly beaten
30g butter, melted and cooled,
   plus extra for cooking

*to serve*
berries
yoghurt
maple syrup

Stir together the lemon juice and milk and leave for 5 minutes. Stir together the flour, baking powder, sugar, eggs, melted butter and a pinch of sea salt. Stir in the milk with lemon juice.

Heat a large non-stick frying pan over medium heat and brush lightly with butter. Use 2–3 tablespoons of batter for each pancake. Cook the pancakes for 2 minutes, until bubbles appear on the surface, then turn over and cook for 1 minute. Keep warm on a plate while you cook the rest. Serve with berries and yoghurt and maybe a drizzle of maple syrup.

**Makes about 12**

# Baked porridge

For this I was inspired by the old-fashioned aristocratic tradition of baking porridge in the Aga overnight.
I don't have the country house, the Aga or the butler to serve me, so this is my 'urban version'. The cream adds indulgence (and you could even serve with a dram of whisky for Scottish authenticity).

135g porridge oats
75g roughly chopped hazelnuts
   (without skins) or pecans
75g roughly chopped dried
   figs or sultanas
1 teaspoon vanilla extract
½ teaspoon ground cinnamon
3 tablespoons soft brown sugar
650ml milk
200ml double cream

*to serve*
stewed fruit

Preheat the oven to 150°C/gas mark 2. Scatter the oats, nuts, dried fruit, vanilla, cinnamon and a pinch of sea salt into a baking dish. Add 1 tablespoon of the sugar and toss it all together. Pour in the milk and cream and bake for 45 minutes.

Sprinkle with the remaining sugar and put back in the oven for another 15 minutes. Serve with stewed fruit.
**Serves 6**

# Hash browns

I've eaten many hotel breakfasts that include poor specimens of the classic American hash brown potatoes — singed, greasy nuggets that were clearly deep-fried from frozen. If you've tasted something similar, please don't let it put you off. These are nothing like that. Crunchy on the outside and light and fluffy inside, they're such a crowd-pleaser that you can make them the main feature of the meal. Serve with spicy roast tomatoes and bacon, or try ham or gravlax (page 182).

700g potatoes, peeled
1 onion
2 eggs, lightly beaten
125ml light-flavoured oil,
    such as sunflower, for frying

*to serve*
**cumin-roasted tomatoes (right)**
**brown sugar bacon (right)**

Coarsely grate the potatoes and onion (you can use a food processor for this), then wrap in a clean tea towel and squeeze out as much water as you can. Put the potato and onion in a large bowl, stir in the eggs and season with plenty of sea salt and ground black pepper.

Heat the oil in a non-stick frying pan over medium–high heat. Drop heaped tablespoons of mixture into the pan and flatten slightly to make 1cm-thick patties. Fry for 2–3 minutes on each side, or until golden brown and crisp. Drain on kitchen paper while you cook the rest, adding a little more oil to the pan when necessary. Serve with cumin-roasted tomatoes and brown sugar bacon.
**Makes 16**

## Cumin-roasted tomatoes

Preheat the oven to 200°C/gas mark 6. Halve 8 tomatoes and put them, cut-side-up, in a large roasting tin. Sprinkle each with a pinch of cumin, paprika, soft brown sugar and chilli flakes. Season and bake for 20–25 minutes.
**Serves 4**

## Brown sugar bacon

Preheat the oven to 200°C/gas mark 6. Lay 8 bacon rashers on a baking tray. Sprinkle with 1 teaspoon soft brown sugar and bake for 20–25 minutes until crisp.
**Serves 4**

# Eggs Benedict

Eggs Benedict always reminds me of the first time I made muffins and how chuffed I was when they turned out just like the ones you buy in the supermarket. I felt smug for days. This is a dish that has an increasing number of variations: ham is traditional, but I also like clean-tasting asparagus with the creamy eggs and hollandaise sauce.

4 eggs, at room temperature
2 muffins (right),
   split in half and toasted
4 slices leg ham or
   12 asparagus spears

*hollandaise sauce*
**3 egg yolks**
**1½ tablespoons lemon juice**
**175g unsalted butter,**
   **melted and kept warm**

Make the hollandaise sauce first. Put the egg yolks, lemon juice and 1 tablespoon of water in a food processor and blitz until smooth. With the motor running, slowly add the warm butter and keep mixing until the sauce is thick and glossy. Season to taste with sea salt and white pepper.

Meanwhile, poach the 4 eggs. Pour 5cm water into a frying pan and place over high heat. When the water boils, turn off the heat and break the eggs carefully into the water. Put a lid on the pan and leave for 3 minutes until the whites are opaque. Lift out with a slotted spoon and drain on kitchen paper.

Put a muffin half on each plate, top with a slice of ham or 3 asparagus spears, and then a poached egg. Spoon hollandaise sauce over the egg and serve immediately.
**Serves 4**

## Muffins

7g sachet (2 teaspoons) instant yeast
½ teaspoon bicarbonate of
   soda (baking soda)
600g strong white bread flour, sifted
2 egg whites
1½ teaspoons sea salt
fine polenta, for dusting

Mix together the yeast, bicarbonate of soda, half the flour and 300ml of lukewarm water. Leave for 5 minutes. Beat the egg whites until stiff and then fold into the dough.

Add the salt to the remaining flour, then gradually add this to the dough. When the dough becomes thick and hard to mix, tip out onto a floured surface. Knead for about 10 minutes, or until smooth and glossy. Put the dough in a bowl, cover with cling film and leave for 1 hour until doubled in size.

Dust a large baking tray with polenta. Roll out the dough to 2cm thick and leave to rest for a few minutes. Using a 7cm pastry cutter, cut out circles and place them on the baking tray (re-roll any scraps). Sprinkle with polenta, cover loosely with cling film and leave for 45 minutes.

Heat a large frying pan over medium heat and brush with a little light-flavoured oil (such as sunflower). Fry the muffins for 6–8 minutes on each side. Cool on a wire rack and then keep in the freezer between sheets of baking paper.
**Makes 12–14**

# No-knead bread with apricot jam

I love the idea of making my own bread, but rarely have time. This incredible no-knead bread was inspired by a recipe in *The New York Times*. Word of it swept the internet, although it seemed difficult to believe that it could work. We coated the loaf in a little polenta and, sure enough, it came out of the oven deliciously aerated and chewy, almost like ciabatta with a sourdough flavour. Now that's what I call an improvement in bread making!

**250g strong white bread flour, sifted**
**250g strong wholemeal bread**
**    flour (or bread mix), sifted**
**1 teaspoon instant yeast**
**2 teaspoons sea salt**
**extra flour and a handful of**
**    fine polenta, for dusting**

*to serve*
**butter**
**apricot jam (right)**

Mix together the flours, yeast and salt in a bowl, then stir in 500ml water. The dough will be wet and sticky. Cover with cling film and leave in a warm place for 12 hours, or until the surface of the dough is dotted with bubbles.

Tip the sticky dough onto a floured surface and sprinkle with more flour. Fold the dough once or twice, sprinkling with flour each time. Cover with cling film and leave for 15 minutes.

Sprinkle a tea towel with flour and polenta. Sprinkle the dough with flour and quickly, gently shape into a ball. Put the dough onto the tea towel and dust with more flour and polenta. Cover with another tea towel and leave for 2 hours, or until doubled in size.

Preheat the oven to 230°C/gas mark 8 and put a large casserole dish, with lid, inside to heat up. Slide your hand under the dough, remove the top tea towel and turn the dough over into the hot dish. Shake the dish to spread the dough (it will even out as it bakes), put the lid on and bake for 30 minutes. Remove the lid and bake for another 15–30 minutes until browned. Leave to cool on a rack.
**Makes 1 loaf**

## Apricot jam

450g apricots, pitted, roughly chopped
200g caster sugar
zest and juice of ½ lemon
1 vanilla pod, halved lengthways

Put the apricots, sugar, lemon zest, juice and vanilla in a heavy-based pan over very low heat. Simmer until the sugar has dissolved.

Turn up the heat and let the jam bubble vigorously for 10–15 minutes until it colours and starts to caramelise. Cool a little before serving, or keep in the fridge in a clean jar.
**Makes about 250g**

# Baked French toast with raspberries

I adore French toast, but, as it has to be fried a couple of pieces at a time, it can turn out very labour intensive and keep you pinned to the stovetop when you should be in the garden chatting to friends and drinking a Bloody Mary. For this version I've used the ingredients for French toast but stolen the method from bread and butter pudding, so the whole dish can go in the oven, leaving you free to mingle.

750ml milk
4 eggs
zest of 1 lemon
1 teaspoon vanilla extract
2 teaspoons softened butter
80ml maple syrup
8–10 slices of day-old bread, crusts
    removed, cut into triangles
100g raspberries
2 tablespoons demerara sugar

*to serve*
yoghurt

Whisk the milk, eggs, lemon zest and vanilla in a large bowl. Generously butter a 24cm round ovenproof dish and drizzle the base with the maple syrup.

Arrange the bread triangles in the dish, tucking the raspberries between the slices as you go (save some raspberries for the top). Pour the batter over the bread, scatter with the remaining raspberries, sprinkle with sugar and leave for 15 minutes.

Preheat the oven to 180°C/gas mark 4. Bake the French toast for 50–60 minutes and serve with yoghurt.
**Serves 8**

# Bran muffins

These American-style muffins have become very popular over the last couple of decades and are an easy standard recipe everyone should have up their sleeve. They freeze brilliantly and make great lunchbox fillers, after-school or work snacks, or guilt-free breakfasts on the run. These are different from the more cake-like versions, and I love their earthy, healthy taste.

180g pitted dates, chopped
zest of 1 orange
65ml orange juice
95g soft brown sugar
125ml light-flavoured oil,
    such as sunflower
125g yoghurt
2 eggs, lightly beaten
150g unprocessed bran
120g plain flour
2 teaspoons baking powder
1 teaspoon ground cinnamon

Preheat the oven to 180°C/gas mark 4 and line a 12-hole muffin tin with paper cases.

Put the dates and 185ml boiling water in a bowl and leave to soak for a few minutes. Meanwhile, put the orange zest and juice, sugar, oil, yoghurt, eggs, bran, flour, baking powder and cinnamon in another bowl. Add the dates and their soaking water and mix together well.

Spoon into the muffin cases and bake for 25–30 minutes, or until a skewer comes out clean when poked into the middle. Cool on a wire rack.

**Makes 12**

# Kedgeree

I like my kedgeree made with smoked trout rather than the traditional haddock. I think it makes it slightly gutsier. Kedgeree is now cropping up on the menu at top restaurants because of its great taste, but it also has a useful modern selling point: it's the perfect brunch dish for when gluten-intolerant friends come over.

1 tablespoon olive oil
25g butter
1 red onion, finely chopped
1 garlic clove, finely chopped
2cm piece of fresh ginger,
    peeled and grated
1 teaspoon curry powder
250g long-grain rice
200g smoked trout fillets,
    boned and flaked

*to serve*
3 hard-boiled eggs, quartered
a handful of coriander leaves
lime wedges
½ cucumber, sliced

Heat the oil and butter in a saucepan over medium heat. Add the onion with a good pinch of salt and cook for 8–10 minutes until soft. Add the garlic, ginger and curry powder and cook for 2 minutes.

Add the rice to the pan and stir to coat in oil. Pour in 500ml water, bring to the boil and then turn down to a simmer. Cover the pan and cook for 15 minutes, or until all the water has been absorbed.

Remove the pan from the heat. Carefully stir in the trout. Serve the kedgeree topped with egg and coriander leaves. Serve the lime and cucumber on the side.

**Serves 4**

# Shakshouka

I think all of us should know how to make a basic, but impressive, fried-egg Sunday brunch. I discovered this while I was looking for a restaurant site. The landlord was from Israel and asked if I'd ever tried 'shakshouka', an Israeli fry-up that sounded right up my street. That night I tried out the recipe and loved it. The spooky thing was that the next day I got chatting to an Israeli cab driver and she, too, suggested I try making it. That time I could say I already had.

1 tablespoon olive oil
1 onion, sliced
2 peppers (green, yellow or red), chopped
1 teaspoon paprika
a pinch of dried chilli flakes
4 ripe tomatoes, chopped
2 eggs

*to serve*
paprika
toasted flatbreads

Heat the oil in a frying pan, add the onion and peppers and cook until softened. Stir in the paprika and chilli flakes and cook for 5 minutes. Add the tomatoes and cook for another 2 minutes. Season with sea salt and black pepper.

With your wooden spoon clear two holes in the mixture. Crack an egg into each one and cook to your liking. Sprinkle with a little paprika and serve with flatbreads.

**Serves 2**

# Tea, coffee and chocolate

My first exposure to chai tea was on the beaches of Goa in what, I guess, were the first pop-up cafés — blankets on the sand. Chai has become a healthy alternative to coffee in recent years, and Lindsay, in our Sydney Darlinghurst restaurant, makes the best, so this is an ode to her. I love the piquant and slightly unexpected flavours of Aztec drinking chocolate: cinnamon, vanilla and chilli — this spicy dark drink really does taste as if it's from a mystical time past.

## Chai tea

1 star anise
10 cloves
6 whole allspice berries, crushed
    with the flat of a knife
1 cinnamon stick
2 cardamom pods, crushed
    with the flat of a knife
1–1.5 litres milk
1 tablespoon loose-leaf tea
2–3 tablespoons sugar,
    plus extra to taste

Put the star anise, cloves, allspice, cinnamon, cardamom, milk, tea and sugar in a pan with 250ml water. Stir over medium heat for 3–5 minutes, or until the chai is hot and the flavours have infused. Check for sweetness, then pour into cups through a fine strainer.
**Serves 4–6**

## White hot chocolate

Stir 625ml milk, 150g chopped white chocolate and 80ml brandy (optional) over medium heat until the chocolate melts and the milk is hot. Pour into glasses and top with grated nutmeg.
**Serves 4**

## Spicy dark chocolate

Put a split red chilli and 250ml water in a pan and bring to the boil. Boil until reduced by half. Strain and keep the water.

Put 500ml milk, 1 split vanilla pod and 1 cinnamon stick in a pan and stir until bubbles appear around the edge. Turn the heat to low and add 150g chopped dark chocolate and 2 tablespoons sugar. Stir until melted and dissolved. Remove from the heat and remove the vanilla and cinnamon. Add the chilli water to your taste and serve.
**Serves 4**

## Coffee

This is best made by an expert with a commercial machine, but if you're at home or in a coffee wasteland, here goes… Bring 500ml water to the boil and then leave to cool for 1 minute. Put 50g freshly coarsely ground coffee in your cafetière. Pour the water over the coffee and leave to sit for 3–5 minutes. Press and pour.
**Serves 4**

My grandmother's generation would never have dreamed of buying biscuits — when they invited friends for afternoon tea they rolled up their sleeves and made their own.

The recipes I've chosen here really do reflect a time of life's simpler pleasures: shortbread and buttery madeleines enjoyed with a cup of coffee as an 11 a.m. pick-me-up; scones and vanilla slice for high tea with friends. Some of the classics just can't be improved on, but my basic jam tart has morphed into more of a fruit-laden crostata — definitely a twenty-first-century upgrade.

Although I like to make my recipes as simple as possible, baking is something that not everyone is immediately good at, so don't despair if it isn't always perfect. Baking is a learnt skill, and I still don't always get it spot on. I entered a village cake competition recently and was disqualified for poor presentation. And there I was thinking my Victoria sponge was rustic and homely!

# Baking

# Chocolate chip and pecan cookies

I've tried hundreds of recipes for chocolate chip cookies and these are definitely my favourite. They have a buttery, nutty, almost French taste, and the pinch of salt and bittersweet dark chocolate make them that little bit more grown-up. I like them golden brown but still slightly soft and chewy in the middle. My daughters like them with a glass of cold milk.

**125g unsalted butter, softened**
**110g soft brown sugar**
**55g white sugar**
**1 egg**
**1 teaspoon vanilla extract**
**150g plain flour**
**½ teaspoon sea salt**
**½ teaspoon baking powder**
**100g dark or milk chocolate,**
   **chopped**
**70g chopped pecans (or walnuts)**

Preheat the oven to 180°C/gas mark 4 and line 2 baking trays with baking paper.

Cream the butter and sugars until fluffy and smooth. Add the egg and vanilla and beat again until smooth. Sift the flour, salt and baking powder into the bowl and mix lightly. Stir in the chocolate and nuts.

Spoon dessertspoons of dough onto the baking trays, leaving space for spreading. Bake for 10–12 minutes until pale golden. Cool on the trays for 2–3 minutes before moving to a wire rack to cool completely.

**Makes 12**

# Brown sugar shortbread

Shortbread always makes me think of my childhood Christmases — I loved that crunch from the granulated sugar sprinkled on top. Some people update these by using different types of flour, but I prefer the more traditional recipe. A bag of these makes a great dinner-party gift (a bit more original than a bottle of wine).

250g unsalted butter
120g soft brown sugar
1 teaspoon vanilla extract
220g plain flour
70g cornflour
50g ground almonds
raw sugar, for sprinkling

Beat the butter and sugar with a pinch of sea salt until pale. Add the vanilla and beat again. Gradually fold in the flour, cornflour and ground almonds until well combined.

Divide the dough in half. Roll out each half between large sheets of baking paper to make a 20cm circle. Put the 2 dough circles, still between their sheets of paper, on baking trays and refrigerate for 10 minutes.

Preheat the oven to 160°C/gas mark 3. Remove the dough from the fridge and take off the top pieces of baking paper. Pinch the edges and score into wedges. Sprinkle with the sugar and bake for 25–30 minutes, or until lightly golden. Cut into wedges while still warm, then leave to cool completely on a wire rack.

**Makes 32 pieces**

# Lemon drizzle loaf

The classic lemon drizzle loaf is taken to even greater heights by the addition of coarse, slightly crunchy polenta (we have London's River Café to thank for introducing us to polenta cake). Throw in a few blueberries to keep the cake moist. A slice of this as an afternoon snack with a strong espresso keeps me going for the rest of the day.

225g unsalted butter, softened
225g caster sugar
3 eggs
100g plain flour
100g ground almonds
100g polenta
2 teaspoons baking powder
zest and juice of 1 lemon
zest and juice of 1 lime
200g blueberries

*lemon drizzle*
juice of 1 lemon
60g icing sugar

Preheat the oven to 180°C/gas mark 4. Grease a 1kg loaf tin and dust with flour, shaking out the excess flour.

Beat together the butter and sugar until light and creamy. Add the eggs one at a time, mixing well after each addition.

Fold in the flour, almonds, polenta, baking powder, and lemon and lime zest and juice. Gently fold in the blueberries.

Spoon the mixture into the tin and bake for 40 minutes. Cover with foil and bake for a further 20 minutes, or until a skewer comes out clean when you poke it into the centre.

Leave to cool slightly in the tin, then turn out onto a wire rack.

To make the lemon drizzle, mix together the lemon juice and sugar. Prick all over the top of the loaf with a skewer, pour the drizzle over the loaf and leave to soak in.

**Makes 1 loaf**

# Brownies

Amazingly — as it seems almost impossible to imagine life without them — chocolate brownies are a relatively new arrival in our kitchens. They flew in from the United States as late as the early nineties. Brownies are fantastically easy to make, but use good-quality chocolate or they can end up too sweet. I sometimes make a topping of half double cream, half melted chocolate to spread over the top, then cut the brownies into tiny squares and serve as petits fours.

350g caster sugar
80g cocoa powder
60g plain flour
1 teaspoon baking powder
4 eggs, lightly beaten
200g unsalted butter, melted
2 teaspoons vanilla extract
200g dark chocolate,
　　roughly chopped

Preheat the oven to 160°C/gas mark 3. Line a 22cm square baking tin with baking paper.

Stir together the sugar, cocoa powder, flour and baking powder in a bowl. Mix in the eggs, butter and vanilla until combined, and then mix in the chocolate. Pour into the tin and bake for 40–45 minutes.

Leave to cool slightly in the tin, then turn out onto a wire rack. Cut into squares to serve.
**Makes 12**

# Plum jam tart

This was inspired by two things: those lovely, cake-like Italian fruit tarts that make the perfect pick-me-up with a cuppa; and memories of childhood jam tarts and the nursery rhyme 'Queen of Hearts'. This is my modern-day version — a very delicious fruit-laden crostata.

100g unsalted butter,
   melted and cooled
90g caster sugar
175g plain flour
25g ground almonds

*plum jam topping*
800g plums, pitted and quartered
110g caster sugar
2 teaspoons cornflour
1 tablespoon orange juice

Preheat the oven to 180°C/gas mark 4 and grease and line a 24cm springform cake tin. To make the pastry, stir together the butter and sugar in a large mixing bowl. Add the flour and a pinch of sea salt and stir to make a soft dough.

Press the dough evenly into the base of the tin with your fingertips. Put the tin on a baking tray and bake for 15–20 minutes, or until the pastry is slightly puffy and golden. Remove from the oven and sprinkle the ground almonds over the pastry base.

Meanwhile, to make the topping, toss together the plums, sugar, cornflour and orange juice. Arrange over the pastry base and return to the oven for 30–40 minutes until cooked through. Leave to cool for 5 minutes before serving. Delicious warm or at room temperature.

**Serves 8–10**

'I like fresh fruit to look and taste like its glorious self. Even for a jammy topping, I can't bear to cook it until it loses shape and texture.'

# Carrot cake

Carrot cake reached our shores in the seventies and started a mini revolution. Could this nutty, cinnamon-spiced cake with its cream cheese frosting actually be good for us? (Or at least better for us than chocolate fudge cake?) It has remained the 'healthy' option for yoga bunnies and weekend exercisers, who feel even more virtuous when pairing it with a soy latte. All that aside, it's the texture of the carroty cake and its earthiness that make it a favourite of mine.

200g plain flour
3 teaspoons baking powder
1 teaspoon ground cinnamon
200g grated carrot
250g soft brown sugar
3 eggs
250ml light-flavoured oil,
    such as sunflower
100g sultanas
100g chopped walnuts
zest of 1 orange

*cream cheese frosting*
250g cream cheese, softened
30g unsalted butter, softened
1 teaspoon vanilla extract
125g icing sugar, sifted

Preheat the oven to 170°C/gas mark 3. Lightly grease and line a 24cm springform cake tin.

Sift the flour, baking powder and cinnamon into a large bowl and stir in the carrot. Make a well in the centre.

Whisk the sugar and eggs in another bowl. Slowly whisk in the oil. Pour the mixture into the well in the dry ingredients and mix until just combined. Fold in the sultanas, walnuts and orange zest.

Pour into the tin and bake for 1–1¼ hours, until a skewer poked into the centre comes out clean. Leave in the tin for 5 minutes before turning out onto a wire rack to cool.

To make the cream cheese frosting, beat the cream cheese, butter and vanilla until smooth. Gradually add the icing sugar and beat until smooth. Spread over the cake.
**Serves 8–10**

# Scones

When I was a child, we would go for drives in the country and seek out the 'Devonshire tea' signs. Today I still crave those scones with their strawberry jam and thick clotted cream. The traditional 'secret' ingredient that our grandmas added for the lightest, best-aerated scones was lemonade. For my modern spin I use sparkling water with a little sugar and lemon juice. The results are just as perfect and there's an added bonus — no rubbing butter into flour with your fingertips.

**3 tablespoons icing sugar**
**450g self-raising flour**
**2 teaspoons baking powder**
**200ml single cream**
**125ml sparkling water**
**2 tablespoons lemon juice**
**milk, for brushing**

*to serve*
**strawberry jam**
**clotted or whipped cream**

Preheat the oven to 200°C/gas mark 6 and dust a large baking tray with flour.

Sift the icing sugar, flour and baking powder into a large bowl. Mix together the cream, water and lemon juice and then quickly add to the bowl and combine with the dry ingredients with a knife. Turn out onto a floured surface, knead very lightly until smooth and press out to about 2–3cm thick.

Use a 5cm cutter or a glass to cut rounds from the dough (re-roll the scraps). Put the scones tightly together on the tray, brush with milk and bake for 10–12 minutes, or until golden and puffed. Serve warm with butter or strawberry jam and clotted cream.
**Makes 20**

## Sultana scones

Add 80g sultanas and 1 teaspoon orange zest when you add the liquid to the dry ingredients.

## Cheese scones

Leave out the icing sugar from the dough and add 75g grated Cheddar cheese and 2 teaspoons finely chopped chives to the dry ingredients.

# Butterscotch madeleines

My love of madeleines was reconfirmed recently by a wonderful dinner at St. John, in London's Smithfield, where a plateful was served, still warm, to finish the meal. They are having a revival at the moment, whether laced with honey or perhaps with old-fashioned butterscotch, as I've done here. I am not normally a stickler, but I do insist you find the proper biscuit tray for these — it is that which gives them their signature shape.

100g unsalted butter
2 tablespoons golden syrup
2 eggs
60g caster sugar
75g plain flour, sifted
1 teaspoon baking powder

*to serve*
icing sugar, to dust

Preheat the oven to 170°C/gas mark 3. Grease a madeleine tray and dust with flour, shaking off the excess.

Melt the butter in a small pan. Remove from the heat, stir in the syrup and leave to cool.

Meanwhile, whisk the eggs, sugar and a pinch of sea salt until pale and fluffy. Add the flour, baking powder and syrup mixture and fold everything together.

Spoon the mixture into the madeleine tray and bake for 8–10 minutes. Cool on a wire rack. Serve dusted with icing sugar.
**Makes about 20**

# Vanilla slice

Vanilla slices were my absolute favourite childhood treat, and I still can't resist them in any incarnation. In France, the equivalent pastry is the millefeuille; in Greece, the galaktoboureko. If you have the skill and tenacity to make your own puff pastry, please go ahead. This recipe uses good-quality ready-rolled, or you could use filo to create a vanilla slice more akin to the galaktoboureko.

two 28cm square sheets
   ready-rolled puff pastry

*vanilla custard*
**750ml milk**
**1 vanilla pod (or 1 teaspoon**
   **vanilla bean paste)**
**9 egg yolks**
**180g caster sugar**
**60g cornflour**

*passion fruit icing*
**185g icing sugar, sifted**
**15g unsalted butter, softened**
**1 tablespoon passion fruit juice,**
   **strained**
**1 tablespoon passion fruit pulp**

Preheat the oven to 220°C/gas mark 7. Line a 20cm square cake tin with 2 lengths of baking paper, so that each side has an overhang of at least 5cm of paper (these will be 'handles' to lift out the finished slice).

Line 2 baking trays with baking paper and put the pastry squares on them. Prick all over with a fork and bake for 10 minutes, then carefully press the pastry with a clean tea towel to push out any air.

Reduce the oven temperature to 200°C/ gas mark 6 and bake the pastry for a further 10–15 minutes, or until golden brown. Press flat with the tea towel again and leave to cool. Trim the pastry to fit the cake tin and lower the first sheet in.

To make the custard, put the milk in a saucepan over medium–high heat. Split the vanilla pod, scrape the seeds into the milk and also throw in the empty pod. Bring just to the boil. Meanwhile, whisk the egg yolks and sugar until thick and pale, then stir in the cornflour.

Pour the hot milk onto the egg mixture in a thin stream, stirring constantly. Strain back into the saucepan and stir for about 10 minutes over medium heat, or until the custard is thick. Take care not to scorch the custard on the bottom of the pan.

Pour the hot custard into the pastry-lined tin. Turn over the second pastry sheet so the flat side is up, place on top of the custard and carefully press in place. Leave to cool.

To make the passion fruit icing, put the sugar in a small bowl and stir in the butter, then stir in the passion fruit juice and pulp. The icing should be thick but spreadable — if it is too thick, add 1 teaspoon warm water. Spread over the pastry and leave to set.

Use the baking paper handles to lift the slice out of the tin. Neaten the sides with a sharp serrated knife, then cut into slices.
**Makes 8–12 pieces**

# Cake for a crowd

There is no longer an excuse for packet cake mix — this basic cake recipe makes opening the packet look tricky. Throw all the ingredients into a bowl and stir together — it'll never let you down. You can turn it into cupcakes, instead, or make a second cake, place them side by side and ice with buttercream to feed an even bigger crowd.

335g plain flour
1 tablespoon baking powder
185g unsalted butter, softened
1–2 teaspoons vanilla extract
220g caster sugar
3 eggs
185ml milk

*vanilla whipped buttercream*
280g icing sugar, sifted
80g unsalted butter, softened
1 teaspoon vanilla extract
1 tablespoon milk

Preheat the oven to 180°C/gas mark 4. Grease and line a 20cm square cake tin.

Sift the flour and baking powder into a large bowl. Add the butter, vanilla, sugar, eggs and milk and beat with electric beaters for 3–4 minutes until smooth.

Pour the mixture into the tin and bake for 40–45 minutes, or until golden brown and a skewer poked into the centre comes out clean. Leave in the tin for 5 minutes, then turn out onto a wire rack to cool completely.

To make the buttercream, beat together all the ingredients with electric beaters on low speed. Then beat for 3–4 minutes on high speed until pale and fluffy. Spread over the cooled cake. Decorate with berries, grated chocolate or candles for the occasion.
**Serves about 20**

## Cupcakes

Line eighteen 80ml muffin holes with paper cases. Spoon the cake mixture into the cases and bake for 15–20 minutes or until they are golden brown and a skewer poked into the centre comes out clean. Leave to cool in the tin for 5 minutes, then turn out onto a wire rack.
**Makes 18**

Soup is the ultimate comfort food — a hearty bowl of something nourishing and spoonable can breathe life back into you like no other dish. There's something so cosy and intimate about soup's warming goodness that every culture seems to have its own classic: French onion and fisherman's bouillabaisse; Malaysian laksa; Thai tom yum; Italian borlotti bean; Russian borscht… Some of my versions are a little cheeky in that I've cut corners to save time and freshened up a few ingredients.

One of the great things about making soup is that you get a lot of bang for your buck; you can use leftovers from the night before, clear out the fridge and use up all the bits in the veggie drawer, or prepare something special for friends. Make a big panful; it can always go in the freezer if you have too much.

However many corners you want to cut, though, nothing beats proper stock made from the bones of a roast from the night before. Maybe that's why soup is so often a Monday-night supper in our house.

# Soup

# Tom yum

Like a spa treatment for your tastebuds, there is definitely something head-clearing about Thailand's tom yum soup. Invigorating as well as soothing, it wakes up both brain and body. And that fragrant hit of kaffir lime leaves (which you can now easily find both dried and frozen) is the perfect antidote to any sluggish feeling.

500ml chicken stock
8 kaffir lime leaves (fresh or dried)
2 red (bird's eye) chillies, halved (deseeded first, if you like)
3cm piece of fresh ginger, peeled and thinly sliced
2 tablespoons fish sauce
1 tablespoon tamarind paste
200g glass (bean thread) noodles or rice vermicelli noodles
150g green beans, topped and cut into short lengths
12 cherry tomatoes
16 large raw king prawns, peeled and deveined with tails left on

*to serve*
lime wedges

Put the stock, lime leaves, chilli, ginger, fish sauce, tamarind paste and 500ml water in a large heavy-based saucepan. Bring to the boil, then reduce the heat to medium–low and simmer for 5 minutes.

Meanwhile, put the noodles or vermicelli in a large heatproof bowl and cover with boiling water. Leave for 3 minutes to soften, then rinse, drain and spoon into serving bowls.

Add the beans to the soup and simmer for another 2 minutes. Add the tomatoes and prawns, then remove from the heat. Leave the soup for 1 minute so the prawns are just opaque and cooked, then ladle over the noodles. Serve with lime wedges.

**Serves 4**

# Tomato soup with cashew and coconut sambal

I'm not usually a fan of purées, but tomato is one soup that just has to be smooth. I grew up on Heinz cream of tomato thinned out with milk, and now I add coconut milk to my own recipe. I think this is a lovely example of just how much my tastes have changed and, at the same time, the important role nostalgia plays in my love of some dishes. A sambal of cashews and coconut livens this up with a good, crunchy contrast.

2kg plum tomatoes, halved
1 red pepper, halved
   and deseeded
6 garlic cloves, peeled
1 small carrot, diced
60ml olive oil
2 teaspoons ground coriander
2 teaspoons ground cumin
a pinch of dried chilli flakes
   (optional)
250ml chicken or
   vegetable stock
125ml coconut milk

*to serve*
**cashew and coconut sambal (right)**

Preheat the oven to 200°C/gas mark 6. Put the tomatoes, red pepper, garlic and carrot in a large casserole dish, drizzle with olive oil, sprinkle with the spices and season with sea salt and ground black pepper. Cover with a lid or foil and bake for 1 hour. Uncover and bake for another 30 minutes, or until the vegetables are well cooked.

Transfer the vegetables to a food processor or blender and mix until smooth.

Return the mixture to the casserole or a large heavy-based saucepan and add the stock and coconut milk. Stir well and cook over medium heat until warmed through. Ladle into serving bowls and serve topped with a little cashew and coconut sambal.
**Serves 4–6**

## Cashew and coconut sambal

50g cashew nuts
20g flaked coconut
a large handful of coriander leaves

Put the cashews, coconut, coriander leaves, a large pinch of sea salt and 60ml water in a blender or food processor and process until roughly chopped.
**Serves 4–6 as an accompaniment**

# Chicken noodle soup

Chicken noodle soup is a traditional favourite food when we're feeling poorly. I find I need a little extra kick in the bowl, even more so when I'm not feeling great. The simple addition of oyster sauce in this recipe gives the soup an unexpected luxuriousness, and serving it with chilli clears the foggiest of heads.

**4 pak choy, shredded crossways**
**250g fresh egg noodles**
**300g shredded poached chicken (right)**
**2 litres chicken stock**
**1 bunch of asparagus,**
**   trimmed and cut in half**
**90ml oyster sauce**
**1½ tablespoons caster sugar**
**3 tablespoons lime juice**

*to serve*
**coriander leaves**
**finely sliced red chilli**
**very finely sliced spring onion**
**lime wedges**

Divide the pak choy among 4 large soup bowls. Put the noodles in a large heatproof bowl, cover with boiling water and soak according to the packet instructions. Drain well and spoon into the bowls. Top with the shredded chicken.

Meanwhile, bring the stock to the boil in a large pan over high heat and blanch the asparagus until bright green and tender but crisp. Lift out with a slotted spoon and add to the bowls. Add the oyster sauce, sugar and lime juice to the stock. Ladle over the noodles and finish with coriander leaves, chilli, spring onion and lime wedges.
**Serves 4**

## Poached chicken breasts

a handful of flat-leaf parsley or coriander
1 tablespoon black peppercorns
2 spring onions or ½ onion, roughly chopped
1 tablespoon sea salt
4 skinless chicken breasts

Put the parsley, peppercorns, spring onions and salt into a large pan filled with cold water and bring to the boil. Add the chicken breasts, turn off the heat, put the lid on the pan and leave the chicken to poach for 1 hour. Remove the chicken from the poaching liquid.
**Serves 4**

# French onion soup

In the seventies my parents' friends would mix a packet of dehydrated French onion soup with cream cheese to make a party dip — which just shows how far food has moved on in recent times! As a true Aussie bloke, I sometimes feel that soup isn't really a 'meal', but the melted gruyère croutons make this rich, savoury dish more than satisfying. The egg yolks make the soup glossy and a little thicker and richer.

80g butter
1.25kg brown onions,
    halved and thinly sliced
1 bay leaf
3 thyme sprigs
1 tablespoon plain flour
125ml white wine
1 litre beef stock
2 egg yolks (optional)
80ml brandy
250g gruyère cheese, grated
1cm-thick slices of baguette,
    lightly toasted

Melt the butter in a large heavy-based pan over medium heat and add the onion, bay leaf and thyme. Cook, stirring occasionally, for about 1 hour, or until the onion is beautifully soft, golden brown and caramelised. Add the flour and cook for 1 minute, stirring constantly. Stir in the wine and simmer, stirring, for 2–3 minutes.

Add the stock and 375ml water. Bring to the boil, then reduce the heat to low and simmer, stirring occasionally, for 30 minutes. Season with sea salt and ground black pepper. Preheat the oven to 200°C/gas mark 6.

Whisk the egg yolks (if using) and brandy into the soup and ladle into 6 ovenproof bowls. Put the bowls on a large baking tray. Sprinkle half the cheese over the top of the soup bowls. Float one or two baguette slices in each bowl and sprinkle with the rest of the cheese. Bake in the oven for 10 minutes until the cheese is melted and bubbling. Serve immediately.
**Serves 6**

# Fish soup with chorizo

I'm tempted to give this the alternative name 'Bill's bastard child of bouillabaisse and paella'. I adore French bouillabaisse, but the addition of spicy chorizo gives this dish a real Spanish flamboyance. Make this a meal with a loaf of garlic bread: mix some softened butter with extra-virgin olive oil, sea salt, black pepper, chopped flat-leaf parsley and a few crushed cloves of garlic. Spread over a sliced (but not all the way through) baguette, wrap in foil and bake at 180°C/gas mark 4 for 20 minutes.

2 tablespoons olive oil
1 onion, finely sliced
1 fennel bulb, trimmed
    and finely sliced
1 chorizo sausage, sliced
4 garlic cloves, crushed
1 teaspoon finely grated fresh ginger
1 red chilli, finely chopped
    (deseeded first, if you like)
a large pinch of saffron threads
½ teaspoon paprika
125ml white wine
400g tin chopped tomatoes
375ml fish or vegetable stock
1 teaspoon caster sugar
1 bay leaf
350–400g white fish fillets,
    cut into small pieces
8 mussels, scrubbed and
    beards removed
8 large raw king prawns, peeled
    and deveined with tails left on
1 tablespoon chopped flat-leaf parsley
lemon juice, to taste

Heat the olive oil in a large heavy-based pan over medium heat. Add the onion, fennel and a good pinch of sea salt and cook, stirring occasionally, for about 5 minutes until softened. Add the chorizo and cook for 2 minutes.

Add the garlic, ginger, chilli, saffron and paprika and cook for 2 minutes until fragrant. Pour in the wine and scrape the bottom of the pan with your wooden spoon to deglaze it. Add the tomatoes, stock, sugar, bay leaf and 250ml water. Season with sea salt and ground black pepper and leave to simmer for 20–25 minutes.

Gently lower the fish, mussels and prawns into the soup, cover the pan and cook for 2–3 minutes until the fish and prawns are just opaque and the mussels have opened (discard any that remain tightly closed after cooking). Check the seasoning, scatter with parsley and add lemon juice to taste.
**Serves 4**

# Laksa

This rich and fragrant noodle soup is fast becoming the 'spaghetti Bolognese' of Australia. When I visited the Northern Territory, the true outback, and saw 'laksa' next to 'meat pie' on the sign outside a rough and ready roadside diner, I realised just how popular it is. Laksa can have an ingredients list as long as your arm, so this is my simplified version for everyday enjoyment. For the sake of my arteries, I use more stock than coconut milk. Instead of tofu, you can use chicken or prawns.

250g rice vermicelli noodles
3–4 tablespoons laksa paste
1 litre chicken stock or water
250ml coconut milk
4 pak choy, leaves separated
   and sliced lengthways
300g silken firm tofu, thickly sliced
150g bean sprouts
2 spring onions, sliced lengthways
1 red chilli, finely sliced lengthways

*to serve*
lime wedges

Put the noodles in a large heatproof bowl and cover with boiling water. Leave for 2 minutes to soften, then rinse and drain well. Spoon into 4 large serving bowls.

Heat a large heavy-based pan over high heat, add the laksa paste and cook, stirring, for 1 minute until fragrant. Add the stock and coconut milk and bring to a simmer. Add the pak choy and tofu and cook for 1 minute or until the pak choy is bright green.

Spoon the soup over the noodles and top with the bean sprouts, spring onion and chilli. Serve with lime wedges.
**Serves 4**

# Vegetable soup

I have a great fondness for green beans. I celebrate summer by putting them into a soup pan and making my quick version of an Italian minestrone primavera. Instead of the traditional macaroni or other small pasta, I throw in some packet ravioli or tortellini to boost this into a colourful one-pot family supper. If everyone's extra-hungry, you can even add the shredded meat from a rotisserie chicken.

2 tablespoons olive oil
1 large onion, chopped
1 fennel bulb, trimmed and chopped
2 garlic cloves, crushed
1.5 litres chicken stock
2 courgettes, diced
200g green beans, topped and
    cut into short lengths
150g peas (fresh or frozen)
400g ravioli or tortellini (I like to use
    the spinach and ricotta variety)

*to serve*
chopped basil
grated Parmesan

Heat the oil in a large heavy-based pan over medium heat. Add the onion and fennel and cook, stirring occasionally, for 5 minutes until softened. Add the garlic and cook, stirring, for 1–2 minutes until fragrant.

Add the stock, courgette, beans and peas and bring to the boil. Reduce the heat and simmer, stirring occasionally, for 5 minutes.

Increase the heat to high and bring the soup to the boil. Add the pasta and simmer for 3–4 minutes, or until the pasta rises to the surface and is cooked through. Season with sea salt and ground black pepper.

Ladle into 4 serving bowls and serve immediately with basil and grated Parmesan.
**Serves 4**

# Spiced butternut squash soup

This soup is a hearty, textured, spice-laden bowlful, mashed together rather than blended, so the flavours melt into each other. I find the smooth, baby food-like texture of traditional butternut squash soup too gluey for my liking. If you cover the dish when you roast the vegetables, they steam and collapse, rather than caramelising, which makes them more soup-friendly.

1.5kg butternut squash,
    peeled, cut into 3cm cubes
750g tomatoes, quartered
6 garlic cloves, peeled
1 small carrot, chopped
60ml olive oil
½–1 teaspoon dried chilli flakes
2 teaspoons ground cumin
2 teaspoons ground coriander
2 teaspoons paprika
1.25 litres vegetable
    or chicken stock
180g red lentils

*to serve*
yoghurt
sumac
crusty bread

Preheat the oven to 180°C/gas mark 4. Put the squash, tomatoes, garlic and carrot in a large flameproof casserole dish, drizzle with olive oil, sprinkle with the spices and season with sea salt and ground black pepper. Cover the dish and bake for 1½ hours, or until the vegetables are soft.

Roughly mash the vegetables with a fork or potato masher and stir in the stock. Put the casserole dish on the stovetop over medium heat and bring the soup to the boil.

Add the lentils, reduce the heat to low and simmer for 15–20 minutes until the lentils are tender. Add a little extra stock or water if the soup becomes too thick. Season and ladle into bowls. Top with a dollop of yoghurt and a sprinkle of sumac and serve with crusty bread.

**Serves 4–6**

# Baked borlotti bean and pancetta soup

I rarely soak beans overnight when I'm cooking at home; I'll use tinned instead. This soup, however, is the exception — it tastes so much better if you make the effort, and the rest is so easy you'll find you can afford the time. (Just about the only other thing you need to do is chop an onion.) I serve this with torn ciabatta croutons spiked with chilli, giving a nod to the traditional Italian ribollita which inspired the recipe.

**375g dried borlotti beans**
**2 red onions, diced**
**100g pancetta, chopped,**
    **or a ham hock**
**6 garlic cloves, thinly sliced**
**4 celery stalks, diced**
**½ teaspoon dried chilli flakes,**
    **plus ½ teaspoon extra**
**2 teaspoons chopped rosemary**
**1 litre chicken or vegetable stock**
**200g ciabatta bread, crust**
    **removed, roughly torn**
**1 tablespoon olive oil**
**1 bunch cavolo nero, shredded**

Put the borlotti beans in a large bowl, cover with cold water and leave to soak for 8 hours or overnight. Rinse the beans under cold running water, then drain well.

Preheat the oven to 180°C/gas mark 4. Put the beans in a large casserole dish with the onion, pancetta or ham hock, garlic, celery, chilli flakes, rosemary, stock and 1 litre water. Season with sea salt and black pepper. Put the lid on the dish and bake in the oven for 2 hours, stirring occasionally, until the beans are tender, adding a little more water if necessary.

When the soup is nearly ready, put the ciabatta on a baking tray, drizzle with olive oil and sprinkle with the extra chilli flakes and some sea salt. Bake for 10–15 minutes until golden brown.

If you used the ham hock, lift it out now, shred the meat and return to the soup with the cavolo nero. Put the lid back on and leave for a couple of minutes until the cavolo nero is bright green. Ladle into bowls and top with the toasted ciabatta croutons.
**Serves 6**

# Beetroot soup

As soon as I started preparing this, on a bleak, grey November day in London, the gorgeous purple-pink colours of the red onion, red cabbage and beetroot completely won me over. It's wonderful to have a burst of colour amid the roasted browns of so many traditional winter foods. I did discover one problem with this lovely dish, though… After I'd tested the recipe, I had to hurry to a meeting in a very chic, very minimalist, very all-white hotel — with very pink hands.

2 tablespoons olive oil
1 red onion, sliced
3 garlic cloves, sliced
5cm piece of fresh ginger,
    peeled and finely sliced
1 teaspoon ground coriander
½ small red cabbage, sliced
600g beetroots, peeled and diced
1.5 litres chicken stock
400g tin chopped tomatoes
1 tablespoon honey

*to serve*
horseradish cream (right)
rye bread

Make the horseradish cream first, as it needs a couple of hours in the fridge.

To make the soup, heat the oil in a large heavy-based saucepan over medium heat. Add the onion and a pinch of sea salt and cook for 10 minutes until softened. Add the garlic, ginger, coriander, cabbage and beetroot, then pour in the stock and stir in the tomatoes and honey. Bring to a simmer and cook for 25 minutes.

Let the soup cool slightly and then purée in batches. Serve with horseradish cream and rye bread.
**Serves 4–6**

## Horseradish cream

200ml double cream
2 tablespoons grated fresh horseradish
1 tablespoon Dijon mustard
1 teaspoon white wine vinegar

Whisk together all the ingredients with a little sea salt and white pepper until the cream just holds its shape. Refrigerate for a couple of hours to let the flavours develop. This also makes a lovely sauce for a perfectly cooked steak (page 165).
**Serves 4–6**

At heart I'll always be a Sydney boy and, whatever the weather, I crave salads. I need that crisp, refreshing, healthy-tasting hit and I find it hard to eat a meal that doesn't have some kind of crunch. It might be just a simple plate of sliced cucumber with a little salt, olive oil, lemon and sugar, or something more elaborate like a salade Niçoise or Middle Eastern fattoush.

Salads of my childhood consisted of iceberg lettuce, tinned beetroot, fridge-cold tomatoes and salad cream. Thank goodness things have changed since then, but I enjoy updating the old classics for our everyday modern life.

Dressings can make or break the deal, of course, and I like to vary the vinegars I use. Balsamic vinegar was one of those ingredients (perhaps along with sun-dried tomatoes) that was a great eighties craze. It has its place but I also love red, white, rice wine and sherry vinegars, each of which brings its own character to the bowl.

# Salads

# Salade Niçoise

My first proper restaurant job was in the Sydney café La Passion du Fruit. The café was run by a talented woman called Chrissy who had an intuitive understanding of Provençal food. I still crave her salade Niçoise — she made it with tinned tuna, but it couldn't have tasted more authentic. This is the deluxe version with fresh tuna, but for a quick lunch I often follow Chrissy's lead and use tinned.

2 x 200g tuna steaks
1 tablespoon olive oil
1 teaspoon fennel seeds, crushed
    with the back of a knife
½ teaspoon dried chilli flakes
2 eggs, at room temperature
100g green beans, topped
100g mixed lettuce leaves
3 radishes, cut into wedges
4 plum tomatoes, cut into wedges,
    or a punnet of cherry tomatoes,
    halved
5 new potatoes,
    boiled and quartered

*anchovy vinaigrette*
4 good-quality anchovy fillets in oil
100ml extra-virgin olive oil
30ml red wine vinegar
1 tablespoon lemon juice

*to serve*
a handful of black olives,
    pitted and halved
a handful of basil leaves
chopped flat-leaf parsley

Heat a griddle pan over medium–high heat. Brush the tuna steaks with the olive oil and scatter with the fennel seeds and chilli flakes. Season with sea salt and ground black pepper. Sear the tuna in the hot pan for 2 minutes on each side (it should still be pink in the middle). Remove the tuna from the pan and leave to rest before slicing.

Put the eggs in a pan of cold water, bring to the boil and boil for 6 minutes. Lift out with a slotted spoon and drop into cold water. When cool, peel and slice the eggs.

Meanwhile, blanch the beans in a pan of lightly salted boiling water for 2–3 minutes until they are bright green and tender yet crisp. Rinse under cold running water and drain well.

For the vinaigrette, pound the anchovies to a rough paste using a mortar and pestle. Stir in the olive oil, red wine vinegar and lemon juice. Season with ground black pepper.

Arrange the eggs, beans, lettuce, radishes, tomatoes, potatoes and tuna on a serving platter and let people help themselves. Drizzle with the anchovy vinaigrette and scatter with the olives, basil and parsley.

**Serves 4**

# Noodle salad with prawns, cashews and mint

This has become a summer staple in our house — it doesn't need any cooking and is perfect when you're feeling too hot and lazy to eat anything stodgy. The noodles and carrot are the only essentials; the rest you can pretty much decide on yourself, as the sweet chilli dressing holds it all together so well. You could throw in shredded chicken instead of the prawns, and iceberg lettuce at the bottom of each dish is a nice touch.

2 tablespoons caster sugar
2 tablespoons rice vinegar
1 large carrot, peeled and
    cut into thin batons
200g rice vermicelli noodles
1 teaspoon light-flavoured
    oil, such as sunflower
24 large cooked prawns, peeled,
    deveined and halved lengthways
1 Lebanese cucumber,
    cut into chunks
a large handful of mint leaves
50g cashew nuts, lightly
    toasted and chopped
chilli dressing (right)

*to serve*
lime wedges

Mix together the sugar and vinegar in a bowl, add the carrot and leave to marinate for 20 minutes.

Put the rice noodles in a large heatproof bowl, cover with boiling water and leave to soak for 2 minutes, or until softened. Rinse under cold running water, drain well and toss with the oil. Season with sea salt.

Drain the carrot and add to the noodles with the prawns, cucumber, mint leaves and cashew nuts.

Add chilli dressing to the salad (as much as you like) and toss gently. Serve immediately, with lime wedges.
**Serves 4–6**

## Chilli dressing

1 red chilli, deseeded and
    roughly chopped
1 green chilli, deseeded and
    roughly chopped
2 garlic cloves, roughly chopped
2 tablespoons soft brown sugar
3 tablespoons fish sauce
3 tablespoons lime juice
2 red Asian shallots, roughly chopped
1 tomato, roughly chopped

To make the dressing, put all the ingredients in a blender and whiz until smooth. This dressing can be stored in the fridge for 2–3 days.
**Serves 4–6**

# Quinoa salad with pomegranate

This pseudo-grain (it's actually a seed) has been a staple in South America for centuries, but more recently it has become a favourite on California-style health-food café menus. Don't let that put you off though! It has a lovely nutty flavour and texture and, like couscous and bulgar wheat, makes a perfect starchy 'canvas' for gutsy salads like this. It's also great for the wheat intolerant, so seems destined to become ever more fashionable.

150g quinoa
150g green beans, topped and
    cut into short lengths
a handful of flat-leaf parsley leaves
2 tablespoons lemon juice
3 tablespoons extra-virgin olive oil
2 Lebanese cucumbers,
    cut into chunks
1 green pepper, deseeded,
    cut into strips
1 small red onion, very finely sliced
100g green olives, pitted
seeds from 1 pomegranate

*to serve*
extra-virgin olive oil
lemon juice

Rinse the quinoa and put in a large pan with 500ml cold water. Bring to the boil, reduce the heat to low, cover the pan and simmer for 12–15 minutes, until all the water has been absorbed.

Meanwhile, blanch the beans in a pan of lightly salted boiling water for 2–3 minutes until they are bright green and tender yet crisp. Rinse under cold running water and drain well.

Put the quinoa in a bowl and stir in the parsley, lemon juice and olive oil. Season with sea salt and ground black pepper. Spoon into serving dishes and top with the cucumber, green pepper, onion, olives and pomegranate seeds. Add a drizzle of olive oil and a squeeze of lemon juice to serve.
**Serves 4**

# Lentil, beetroot and celery fattoush with labna

Here I've played around with a traditional lentil salad, making it more like a fattoush with crunchy torn flatbreads, and adding one of my favourite curd cheeses, labna. Labna is made from yoghurt and so has a wonderfully tart quality (worthy substitutes would be tangy goat's curd or fromage frais). Earthy, herby and wholesome, this salad works equally well as a main course or as an accompaniment to, say, barbecued lamb cutlets marinated in sliced garlic, cumin and chilli flakes.

2 flatbreads
200g Puy lentils
1 tablespoon extra-virgin olive oil
1 small red onion, finely sliced
1 tablespoon red wine vinegar
a handful of mint leaves
a handful of flat-leaf parsley
    leaves or micro herbs
3 celery stalks, cut into batons

*to serve*
8 roasted and peeled baby
    beetroots (right)
200g labna, or other soft
    white cheese
sumac
extra-virgin olive oil

Roast your beetroots first, as they take a little longer to cook. Use the warm oven to heat the flatbreads for 10–12 minutes until crisp. Leave to cool, then roughly break the bread into pieces.

Put the lentils in a large saucepan with 375ml water and bring to the boil, then reduce the heat and simmer for 15 minutes. Strain the lentils and put in a large bowl. Add the olive oil, onion and vinegar and season with sea salt and ground black pepper. Stir in the mint, parsley and celery.

To serve, spoon the lentil salad into bowls and top with some beetroot, pieces of toasted flatbread and chunks of labna. Sprinkle with a little sumac and drizzle with olive oil.
**Serves 4–6**

## Roasted baby beetroots

8 baby beetroots, unpeeled
1 tablespoon olive oil

Preheat the oven to 220°C/gas mark 7. Put the beetroots in a small baking dish, drizzle with the oil and season with sea salt and ground black pepper. Cover with foil and roast in the oven for 25–30 minutes, or until the beetroots are tender when pierced with a knife. Leave to cool.

Peel the beetroots by rubbing the skin gently with your hands until it comes away. Slice each beetroot in half or into wedges.
**Serves 4–6**

# Bill's everyday green salad

We all now know that we should be eating our five servings of fruit and veg every day. Natalie always worries that our girls haven't had their quota. This is my answer: a crunchy green salad, which I put on the table nearly every night as a precursor to dinner. In the colder months, when the more bitter-tasting leaves are in season, I make a mustard vinaigrette to beef things up. Inès always needs to 'fix' her dressing so it's just the way she likes it. A girl after my own heart!

150g green beans, topped
1 fennel bulb, trimmed
   and finely sliced
2 celery stalks, cut into batons
½ cucumber, peeled and
   cut into batons
1 head of lettuce, leaves torn

*to serve*
extra-virgin olive oil
lemon juice

Blanch the beans in a pan of lightly salted boiling water for 2–3 minutes until they are bright green and tender yet crisp. Rinse under cold running water and drain well.

Arrange the fennel, celery, cucumber and lettuce in a shallow bowl with the beans. Drizzle with olive oil and a squeeze of lemon juice. Season with sea salt and ground black pepper and serve immediately.
**Serves 4**

## Mustard vinaigrette

Whisk together 1 teaspoon Dijon mustard, 2 tablespoons red wine vinegar and 3 tablespoons extra-virgin olive oil. Season with sea salt and ground black pepper.
**Serves 4**

# Thai beef salad

The first time I tried this I felt as though my mouth had experienced a flavour revolution. With its addictive balance of spicy, salty, sweet and sour, this dish is a perfect showpiece for Thai flavours. I use it now as a great way to make a steak go further. Try it with steamed rice, or perhaps a second course of chicken curry (page 138) for a celebration meal.

2 tablespoons oyster sauce
1 tablespoon fish sauce
1 tablespoon caster sugar
1 teaspoon sesame oil
2 x 300g rump steaks
1 lemon grass stalk,
   crushed with the back of
   a knife and finely sliced
1 green chilli, finely chopped
   (deseeded first, if you like)
1 garlic clove, finely chopped
1 tablespoon soft brown sugar
4 tablespoons fish sauce
4 tablespoons lime juice
½ cabbage, cut into wedges
a handful of mint leaves
a handful of coriander leaves
½ cucumber, cut into chunks
1 small red onion, thinly sliced

Mix together the oyster sauce, fish sauce, caster sugar and sesame oil in a large bowl. Add the steaks, turn to coat them well and leave to marinate for 5–10 minutes.

Meanwhile, make the dressing by mixing together the lemon grass, chilli, garlic, brown sugar, fish sauce and lime juice. Arrange the cabbage, mint, coriander, cucumber and red onion on serving plates.

Heat a griddle pan over high heat. When very hot, add the steaks and sear for 2 minutes on each side. Transfer to a warm plate, cover loosely with foil and leave to rest for 5 minutes.

Finely slice the steaks and drape over the salad. Drizzle with the dressing.
**Serves 4**

# Tomato salad with burrata and basil oil

It takes only a couple of great ingredients to make a perfect dish. This simple pairing of juicy tomatoes and creamy burrata (ingredient du jour) needs just a drizzle of aromatic olive oil whizzed up with a handful of basil. I don't often shop at farmers' markets — too many children to wrangle — but they're the perfect place to find the freshest ingredients, as well as interesting varieties of tomato. We used heirloom tomatoes here. Just add a crusty baguette and you're good to go.

2 slices of great bread, such as
   sourdough, torn into small pieces
extra-virgin olive oil
1 garlic clove, crushed
300g top-quality ripe tomatoes, cut into
   small wedges, or halved if small
basil oil (right)
125g ball burrata or mozzarella cheese

*to serve*
basil leaves (green or purple)

Preheat the oven to 180°C/gas mark 4. Lay the bread pieces on a baking tray, drizzle with olive oil and scatter with the crushed garlic. Season with sea salt and ground black pepper and bake for about 15 minutes until golden brown.

Arrange the tomatoes on a serving platter. Season with sea salt and pepper, drizzle with the basil oil and top with torn burrata or mozzarella and the toasted bread. Scatter with basil leaves to serve.

**Serves 4**

## Basil oil

a handful of basil leaves
80ml extra-virgin olive oil

Blanch the basil leaves in boiling water for 10 seconds, then rinse under cold running water. Drain well and squeeze as dry as you can with your hands. Pulse in a blender or food processor with the oil and a pinch of sea salt until well mixed.

**Makes 125ml**

# Coleslaw

Regular readers will know that I always find an excuse to include a 'slaw. Maybe it's the buried memory of a youthful guilty pleasure... those little fast-food tubs of coleslaw! Another (not so enticing) memory is of the 'mayonnaise' my mother, and every other seventies cook, made to coat her coleslaw: mustard powder, vinegar and condensed milk, all boiled up. It tasted just like it sounds! I serve this winter coleslaw with roast pork or duck; and summer 'slaw with every barbecue.

½ red cabbage, finely shredded
75g currants
1 tablespoon caster sugar
3 tablespoons red wine vinegar
3 tablespoons extra-virgin olive oil
2 tablespoons pine nuts
1 onion, finely chopped
1 dried chilli, crumbled
2 tablespoons chopped flat-leaf parsley

In a large salad bowl, mix together the cabbage, currants, sugar, red wine vinegar and 2 tablespoons of the olive oil. Season with sea salt and ground black pepper and set aside to soften for at least 1 hour and up to 3 hours.

Meanwhile, put a non-stick pan over low heat and gently toast the pine nuts. Remove the nuts from the pan and set aside. Heat the remaining olive oil in the pan, turn the heat to low and add the onion and dried chilli. Cook very slowly, stirring occasionally, for about 45 minutes, or until caramelised.

Sprinkle the chilli onion, toasted pine nuts and parsley over the 'slaw and serve.
**Serves 4**

## Classic summer 'slaw

Place ½ shredded savoy cabbage, 1 sliced red onion, 2 tablespoons rinsed capers and a small handful of chopped flat-leaf parsley in a large bowl. In a separate bowl whisk together 4 tablespoons mayonnaise, 2 tablespoons lemon juice and 1 tablespoon white wine vinegar. Toss the 'slaw with the dressing and season with sea salt and ground black pepper.
**Serves 4**

# Caesar salad

Caesar salad has become one of our most popular culinary basics. I love the story that it was invented by Caesar Cardini in his hotel in San Diego in the 1920s, one weekend when they ran short of supplies. (I like a chef's challenge!) The legendary dressing and torn bread croutons fried in butter and garlic are what make this dish.

60g butter
3 garlic cloves, crushed
6 thick slices of sourdough bread, torn into bite-size pieces
40g finely grated Parmesan
leaves of 3 baby cos lettuces
a large handful of flat-leaf parsley leaves
50g shaved Parmesan

*dressing*
1 egg, at room temperature
6 good-quality anchovy fillets in oil, mashed
1 teaspoon tiny salted capers, rinsed and finely chopped
1 tablespoon lemon juice
1 teaspoon Dijon mustard
100ml extra-virgin olive oil

Preheat the oven to 200°C/gas mark 6. Put the butter and garlic in a pan and heat gently until the butter has melted. Add the bread and toss to coat with the butter. Transfer the bread to a large baking tray and season with sea salt. Bake in the oven for 8–10 minutes, or until golden brown. Toss with the grated Parmesan and set aside to cool.

Meanwhile, to make the dressing, put the egg in a pan of cold water, bring to the boil and boil for 3 minutes. Lift out with a slotted spoon and drop into cold water. When the egg is cool, peel and roughly chop (the yolk should still be a little soft).

Stir together the egg, anchovies, capers, lemon juice and mustard. Season to taste. Whisk in the olive oil in a slow, steady stream until you have a thick dressing.

Arrange the lettuce, bread croutons, parsley and Parmesan shavings on a serving plate and drizzle with dressing. Serve immediately.
**Serves 4–6**

# Potato salad

I like to use waxy, yellow new potatoes for this — I find they have a good flavour and hold their shape well when cooked. They also celebrate the fact that our choice of potato varieties is now greater than just 'washed' or 'unwashed'. Depending on my mood, I sometimes like a fresh alternative to the mayo-rich classic. In the variation here, the crunch of radish and slight bitterness of parsley and celery leaves really work well with the earthiness of the potatoes.

1kg new potatoes, scrubbed
    but unpeeled
6 spring onions, chopped
2 celery stalks, chopped
1 tablespoon tiny salted capers, rinsed
a small handful of roughly
    chopped flat-leaf parsley
a small handful of finely chopped dill
100g mayonnaise (right)
juice of ½ lemon

Cook the potatoes in boiling salted water until tender. Drain, leave until cool enough to handle and then slice thickly.

Gently mix the potatoes with the spring onion, celery, capers, parsley and dill. Fold in the mayonnaise and season with sea salt, black pepper and lemon juice to taste.
**Serves 4–6**

## Mayonnaise

4 egg yolks
50ml white wine vinegar
1 teaspoon Dijon mustard
200ml light-flavoured oil, such as sunflower

Put the egg yolks, vinegar and mustard in a food processor or blender and mix until well combined. With the motor running, start to add the oil very slowly (about 1 tablespoon at a time) until the mayonnaise is thick and creamy. Add 1–2 tablespoons hot water if it's too thick. Season to taste with sea salt and ground black pepper. Keep in a sterilised jar in the fridge.
**Makes about 250g**

## Potato salad with radish, parsley and celery leaves

Mix together 4 tablespoons extra-virgin olive oil, 2 tablespoons red wine vinegar and 4 chopped anchovies in a bowl. Season with ground black pepper. Add 1kg still-warm boiled potatoes and stir together gently. Leave to cool to room temperature, then stir in 2 finely chopped celery stalks, a small handful of chopped celery leaves, a small handful of chopped flat-leaf parsley, 4 sliced spring onions and 6 sliced radishes. Garnish with whole flat-leaf parsley leaves to serve.
**Serves 4–6**

Let's face it, life without carbohydrates just isn't much fun. They have the power to refuel and comfort us like no other foods and are the easiest way to create a meal for two or ten. A pack of good-quality dried pasta, a few handfuls of arborio rice or some oven-warmed flatbreads can help even one or two ingredients go a lot further, so in a way carbs are the ultimate in cheap chic. Unless you're making lobster risotto, of course, in which case they're just chic.

Everyone has a favourite pasta sauce that becomes the basic for time-poor midweek suppers or even quick dinner for friends. I remember when my mother first discovered, and subsequently became obsessed with, pesto. We had it almost every other night. Some would call it overkill but, as the other option was spaghetti Bolognese from a tin, I was happy with the deal.

Noodles can be even easier to prepare than pasta — the flavours adjusted at the table to suit everyone's tastes. A big tangled, slippery bowl of Thai pad see ew certainly keeps our family quiet for a while, which is no mean feat.

# Rice, pasta & bread

# Saffron risotto with lobster

Risotto, whether stirred like this or baked in the oven, is a great everyday basic everyone should master. A plain saffron risotto makes a lovely aromatic accompaniment for a casserole instead of potatoes or pasta (you might then leave out the lemon zest and chives). I've added lobster here, for the ultimate celebration dinner. I don't have the heart to throw live lobsters straight into the pot, so I buy mine already 'dealt with'. You can replace the lobster with fresh crabmeat.

50g butter
1 tablespoon olive oil
1 onion, finely chopped
½ fennel bulb, finely chopped
2 garlic cloves, finely chopped
500g arborio rice
200ml white wine
a large pinch of saffron threads
1.5 litres fish or vegetable
    stock, simmering
1 lobster, cooked, flesh removed
    from shell and roughly chopped
zest of 1 lemon
2 tablespoons finely chopped chives
1 tablespoon finely chopped dill

*to serve*
lemon wedges

Heat half the butter with the olive oil in a large heavy-based pan. Once the butter has melted, add the onion and fennel with a good pinch of sea salt and cook gently until softened. Add the garlic and cook gently until fragrant.

Add the rice to the pan and stir well with a wooden spoon to coat all the grains. When the rice has become translucent, add the white wine and stir until absorbed.

Add the saffron to the simmering stock and start adding to the rice one ladleful at a time. Stir constantly and don't add the next ladle of stock until the last one has been absorbed. Keep going for about 20 minutes, or until the rice is cooked and has a loose and creamy texture. Every risotto is different, so you may not need all the stock, or you may use it all up and have to add a little water — either is fine, as long as the rice is al dente.

Stir in the remaining butter, most of the lobster and the lemon zest. Season generously with sea salt and black pepper, put the lid on the pan and leave the risotto to sit for a minute or two. Top with the remaining lobster, chives and dill and serve with lemon wedges.
**Serves 8–10**

# Singapore fried noodles

Strangely, this noodle dish is not from Singapore: it was created by Chinese chefs in Hong Kong. The subtle curry notes combine with the chilli- and soy-enhanced Asian flavours, and it was one of my first forays into spicy food as a child. I always like to have some extra chopped chilli and soy sauce on the table for those who enjoy this with added punch. If you don't have dark soy sauce, add an extra tablespoon of regular soy and an extra teaspoon of brown sugar.

60ml chicken stock
2 tablespoons dark soy sauce
　　or kecap manis
1 teaspoon soft brown sugar
250g rice noodles
3 tablespoons light-flavoured
　　oil, such as sunflower
3 eggs, lightly beaten
200g large raw prawns, peeled
　　and deveined with tails left on
2 teaspoons curry powder
1 onion, finely sliced
5cm piece of fresh ginger,
　　peeled and finely grated
1 green pepper,
　　cut into thin strips
½ cabbage, finely shredded

*to serve*
1 red chilli, finely sliced
　　(deseeded first, if you like)
1 spring onion, finely sliced
　　on the diagonal
a handful of coriander leaves

To make the sauce, mix together the chicken stock, soy sauce and brown sugar and set aside. Soak the noodles in hot water for 2 minutes to soften, then drain well.

Heat a wok over high heat. Add 1 tablespoon of the oil and, when hot, add the eggs and season with sea salt and pepper. Cook for 2–3 minutes, stirring gently to scramble. Remove from the wok and set aside.

Heat another tablespoon of oil in the wok. Add the prawns and cook for 2 minutes. Remove and set aside.

Heat the remaining oil in the wok. Stir-fry the curry powder, onion and ginger for 1 minute. Add the green pepper and stir-fry for 2 minutes. Add the cabbage and stir-fry until wilted.

Add the sauce, noodles, egg and prawns to the wok and stir-fry for 1–2 minutes until heated through. Spoon into bowls and top with chilli, spring onion and coriander.
**Serves 4**

# Spaghetti with scallops and preserved lemon

Classic seafood pasta is usually a very simple combination of seafood, a little wine, olive oil, perhaps butter and some aromatics. A recipe for curried scallops by Simone Beck, who co-wrote *Mastering the Art of French Cooking* with Julia Child, inspired me here. The classic curry flavour she uses, along with the preserved lemon, really emphasises the sweetness of the scallops.

200g spaghetti or angel hair pasta
    or squid-ink long pasta
2 tablespoons olive oil
200g scallops, with or without roes
1 teaspoon curry powder
2 garlic cloves, thinly sliced
1 red chilli, finely chopped
    (deseeded first, if you like)
250ml dry white wine
40g butter
1 tablespoon finely sliced
    preserved lemon
a small handful of finely
    chopped flat-leaf parsley

Cook the pasta in a large pan of lightly salted boiling water until al dente.

Meanwhile, heat 1 tablespoon of the oil in a large frying pan. Toss the scallops in the curry powder and then add to the pan and sear for a minute, turning once. Remove from the pan and set aside.

Put the frying pan back over medium–low heat and add the remaining olive oil. Add the garlic and chilli and cook, stirring, for 1 minute, or until light golden. Add the wine and half the butter, increase the heat to high and boil for 5 minutes.

Return the scallops to the pan. Stir in the preserved lemon and check the seasoning. Remove from the heat.

Drain the pasta well and add to the pan with the scallops. Return to medium heat and stir gently to coat the pasta with sauce. Stir in the parsley and remaining butter and season with black pepper before serving.

**Serves 2**

# Nasi goreng

It says a lot about my Australian background that fried rice is my ultimate comfort food. It brings back memories of the woks of street vendors on my first trips to Thailand and Singapore. I lace my nasi goreng with lots of fresh chilli and probably use less oil than many versions you'll find. I also add piles of fresh ingredients on the side. This is just as good for curing afternoon hunger pangs as it is with a cold beer in the evening.

2 tablespoons light-flavoured
   oil, such as sunflower
6 red Asian shallots, finely chopped
4 garlic cloves, crushed
3 small green chillies, finely chopped
   (deseeded first, if you like)
2 tablespoons kecap manis
2 tablespoons soy sauce
1 teaspoon sugar
700g cooked rice
4 eggs

*to serve*
a handful of shredded iceberg lettuce
½ cucumber, cut into wedges
2 tomatoes, cut into wedges
lemon or lime wedges
Chinese chilli sauce (optional)

Heat your wok over high heat. Add half the oil and, when hot, add the shallots, garlic and chilli and cook, stirring, until softened. Stir in the kecap manis, soy sauce and sugar. Add the rice and stir-fry, moving it around continuously with your spatula, until lightly coloured and heated through.

Meanwhile, heat the remaining oil in a non-stick frying pan over medium–high heat and fry the eggs for 2 minutes, or until they are as runny or firm as you like them.

Serve the fried rice with an egg on top, and lettuce, cucumber, tomatoes and lemon wedges on the side. Add Chinese chilli sauce if you like an extra kick.

**Serves 4**

# Baked orecchiette with sausage and cavolo nero

This is the simplest pasta bake, but the classy ingredients trick people into thinking it's something rather complicated. Use spicy Italian sausage if you like, but I quite enjoy a plain, maybe slightly garlicky, coarse-cut variety. The fennel seed and chilli add a lovely piquant edge and the ricotta melts down to dress the other ingredients. This is my perfect dinner with a glass of red after a long wintery walk…

400g orecchiette pasta
200g cavolo nero, trimmed and leaves torn
1 tablespoon olive oil, plus extra to drizzle
1 red onion, sliced
2 garlic cloves, sliced
½ teaspoon dried chilli flakes
½ teaspoon fennel seeds
4 sausages (the coarsest you can find), meat removed from casings
200g ricotta
a small handful of grated Parmesan

Cook the pasta in a large pan of boiling salted water until al dente. Add the cavolo nero for the last 30 seconds to blanch it, then drain and tip into a baking dish. Preheat the oven to 180°C/gas mark 4.

Heat the oil in a frying pan over medium heat, add the onion and garlic with a pinch of sea salt and fry for 2–3 minutes. Add the chilli flakes and fennel seeds and fry for 10 seconds. Add the sausage and cook, stirring, for 5 minutes until browned.

Add the sausage mixture to the pasta in the dish and stir together. Dot the ricotta over the top and scatter with Parmesan. Drizzle with a little extra olive oil and bake for 10–15 minutes.

**Serves 4**

'Cooking pasta for a crowd is never
as easy as it sounds — you need a huge
pan and a vigilant eye on the clock.
This is when baked pasta dishes come
into their own.'

# Pad see ew

To 'pad Thai' or to 'pad see ew'? That was the question. I've chosen to feature the latter in this book for one main reason: Russ, who has worked at bills for many years, buys pad see ew almost every day for his lunch from the local Thai takeaway. He's worked at plenty of top-class restaurants, including Sally Clarke's in London, but this is his favourite fast-food fix.

2 tablespoons light-flavoured
   oil, such as sunflower
3 garlic cloves, crushed
150g pork or chicken fillet, sliced
2 tablespoons light soy sauce
1½ tablespoons dark soy sauce
1 tablespoon caster sugar
300g Chinese broccoli (gai larn),
   chopped, leaves and stems separated
2 eggs
300g fresh flat rice noodles, cut
   into 3cm-wide noodles

*to serve*
white pepper,
   freshly ground if possible
fish sauce
pickled chilli

Heat your wok over medium–high heat. Add the oil and, when hot, stir-fry the garlic. Add the meat and stir-fry for 3 minutes.

Add the light and dark soy sauces and the sugar and then stir in the broccoli stems. Cook for a couple of minutes and then make a hole in the middle and crack in the eggs. Cook for a few minutes, scraping the eggs with a spatula every few seconds to break them up.

Add the noodles to the wok, using the spatula to move them around and coat them with the sauce but trying not to break them up. Add the broccoli leaves and cook until tender and bright green.

Remove from the heat, season with white pepper and serve with the fish sauce and pickled chilli on the side.
**Serves 2**

# Bolognese sauce

There are almost as many recipes for this classic ragù as there are cooks. It should be soft and almost creamy, the tomatoes more subtle than overpowering. I turned first to the doyenne of Italian cooking, Marcella Hazan, when making Bolognese. She adds milk first, then wine, evaporating one before adding the next. Later, I discovered Mario Batali's time-saving technique of adding both at the same time, and I haven't looked back, being the time-poor kitchen cheat that I am.

2 tablespoons olive oil
20g butter
1 large onion, finely chopped
2 carrots, finely diced
2 celery stalks, finely diced
75g pancetta, diced
350g pork mince
350g beef mince
250ml milk
200ml white wine
800g tinned chopped tomatoes
250ml chicken stock or water

*to serve*
**500g tagliatelle or spaghetti, cooked
grated Parmesan**

Heat the oil and butter in a large heavy-based pan. Add the onion, carrot, celery and pancetta and cook, stirring occasionally, for 5–6 minutes until soft.

Add the pork and beef mince and cook, stirring, for 5–6 minutes until the mince is cooked through, breaking up any lumps with your wooden spoon. Season with sea salt and ground black pepper. Add the milk and wine and cook, stirring occasionally, until they have evaporated. Add the tomatoes and chicken stock and turn the heat to low.

Cook the Bolognese on the barest simmer for 2–3 hours, stirring occasionally and adding a little more stock or water if it becomes dry. Check the seasoning again before serving with pasta and Parmesan.
**Serves 4 (with leftover sauce for another meal)**

## Polenta Bolognese gratin

Bring 1 litre water, 500ml milk and a large pinch of sea salt just to the boil in a large saucepan. Reduce the heat immediately to a simmer and gradually whisk in 375g instant polenta. Stir constantly for 5–6 minutes, or until the polenta is no longer grainy. Remove from the heat, stir in 50g grated Parmesan and season to taste.

Preheat the oven to 180°C/gas mark 4 and lightly oil a baking dish. Spread two-thirds of the polenta over the base of the dish, top with a generous layer of your Bolognese sauce, then spoon the rest of the polenta over the top. Sprinkle with 50g grated Parmesan and drizzle with a little olive oil. Bake in the oven for 20–25 minutes, or until golden.
**Serves 6**

# My spaghetti carbonara

We usually think of carbonara as an age-old Roman dish, but it was apparently created in Italy after the Second World War, using bacon and eggs supplied by American troops. You might prefer your carbonara American-style with cream or Italian-style without — both have champions in our household. A good pancetta (slightly spicy, if you can find it) is essential. I sometimes add a couple of handfuls of frozen peas while I'm cooking the pasta.

**400g spaghetti or conchiglie**
**1 tablespoon olive oil**
**150g pancetta or good bacon, diced**
**4 spring onions, sliced**
**2 garlic cloves, crushed**
**a pinch of dried chilli flakes**
**2 eggs, lightly beaten**
**2 tablespoons crème fraîche**
**40g Parmesan, grated,**
   **plus extra to serve**

Cook the pasta in a large pan of lightly salted boiling water until al dente. Meanwhile, heat the olive oil in a frying pan over medium heat and cook the pancetta until just beginning to brown. Add the spring onion, garlic and chilli flakes and cook, stirring, for a few more minutes.

Mix the eggs, crème fraîche and Parmesan together with plenty of ground black pepper.

Drain the pasta and return to the hot pan. Toss with the pancetta mixture and then stir in the egg mixture (the heat of the pasta and the pan will lightly cook the eggs). Serve immediately.
**Serves 4**

## Classic carbonara

While your pasta is cooking, heat 60ml olive oil in a frying pan and cook the pancetta until browned. Meanwhile, beat 2 eggs in a bowl. Drain the pasta, keeping a tablespoon or two of cooking water. Put the pasta back in the hot pan, add the pancetta and its oil, the eggs and lots of ground black pepper and grated Parmesan. Stir to coat well, adding a little cooking water if you need it, and serve immediately.
**Serves 4**

# Tomato pasta sauce

I might not be known for my green fingers, but I *can* grow cherry tomatoes. This ultra-simple summer pasta makes perfect use of my crop. The tomatoes and garlic are just softened and then stirred into pasta — and that's it! You could add a tin of tuna in olive oil and a big handful of chopped parsley or rocket, if you really wanted to push the boat out. When it's cold outside I like a traditional cooked tomato sauce. Amatriciana is my favourite: satisfyingly savoury with a touch of heat.

## Summer tomato pasta

200g of your favourite pasta
60ml extra-virgin olive oil
2 garlic cloves, grated
1 red chilli, deseeded and
    finely chopped
250g cherry tomatoes, halved
zest of ½ lemon
a handful of basil leaves, torn

Cook the pasta in a large pan of lightly salted water until al dente. Meanwhile, heat the olive oil in a frying pan over low heat and fry the garlic and chilli until fragrant. Add the tomatoes and lemon zest and cook gently for 2–3 minutes, or until the tomatoes begin to soften. Season with sea salt and black pepper. Remove from the heat and stir in the basil leaves. Drain the pasta, toss with the sauce and serve immediately.

**Serves 2**

## Bucatini all'Amatriciana

1 tablespoon olive oil
200g pancetta, rind removed,
    roughly chopped
1 large onion, diced
a large handful of finely
    chopped flat-leaf parsley
½ teaspoon dried red chilli flakes
2 tablespoons red wine vinegar
800g tinned chopped tomatoes
1 teaspoon caster sugar
400g bucatini

Heat the olive oil in a frying pan over medium–high heat, add the pancetta and cook for 10 minutes, stirring occasionally. Add the onion, season well and cook for 5 minutes. Add the parsley and chilli flakes, stir for 5 seconds, then add the vinegar and cook for 30 seconds until it has evaporated.

Add the tomatoes and sugar, bring to the boil, then reduce the heat to a simmer for about 25 minutes, or until the oil separates from the tomato sauce.

Meanwhile, cook the pasta in a large pan of lightly salted boiling water until al dente. Drain, toss with the sauce and serve immediately.

**Serves 4**

# Flatbreads

This recipe made it onto Goop, Gwyneth Paltrow's blog, which I bragged about for days — and, here we go, I'm still bragging! Like anything home-made, these definitely have the edge over shop-bought. I like to barbecue them ('Of course… he is Australian,' I hear you say) and serve with toppings of both the Italian pizza and the Turkish kind. I also use them to mop up curries or eat with kebabs and dips. Try them sprinkled with sesame or fennel seeds, or chilli flakes and oregano.

400g plain flour
2 teaspoons sea salt, plus
    extra to sprinkle
1 teaspoon instant yeast
2 tablespoons olive oil,
    plus extra to brush

Sift the flour and salt into a large bowl and make a well in the centre. Stir the yeast and olive oil into 330ml lukewarm water and pour into the well in the dry ingredients. Mix to form a soft but firm dough.

Transfer the dough to a lightly floured surface and knead for about 5 minutes until smooth and elastic. Put the dough in a lightly oiled bowl, cover with cling film and leave to rise in a warm place for 45 minutes.

Knock back the dough by punching it with your fist. Divide it into 6 even balls and roll each ball into an oval about 5mm thick.

Preheat a barbecue chargrill plate to hot. Brush each flatbread with olive oil and cook on the barbecue for 2–3 minutes, turning once. If you don't have a barbecue, bake in a 220°C/gas mark 7 oven for 20–25 minutes. Sprinkle with sea salt before serving.
**Makes 6**

## Barbecued flatbreads with merguez, caramelised onion and feta

While the dough is rising, put 2 tablespoons olive oil and 1kg sliced onions in a heavy-based pan over medium heat and cook for 20 minutes, stirring occasionally.

Add 1 tablespoon soft brown sugar, 2 tablespoons balsamic vinegar and sea salt and pepper. Cook for another 5 minutes, or until the onion is soft and caramelised. Leave to cool.

Barbecue the 6 flatbreads on one side, then turn and top with the caramelised onion and 2 chopped merguez sausages. Cook again, with the lid closed if your barbecue has one, for 2–3 minutes until the bases are browned. Sprinkle with crumbled feta and chopped flat-leaf parsley and serve with lemon wedges. I sometimes intensify the flavour by spreading the flatbreads with sun-dried tomato paste or pesto before adding the toppings.
**Serves 6**

I've collected a lot of basic chicken recipes over the years and most of them are true family favourites. I can't make lemon chicken without thinking of my grandmother, as it's still her preferred order in any Chinese restaurant; roast chicken is my wife Natalie's signature dish whenever it's her night to cook; and a fragrant Vietnamese-style curry is my version of a Jewish mother's chicken noodle soup — whatever sort of day I've had, it leaves me feeling all is well with the world.

What on earth did we eat before we ate chicken? My father recently reminded me that, amazingly, chicken used to be served only for Christmas or special occasions. And one of the (few) facts I remember from school history is that the French king Henry IV promised his peasants 'a chicken in the pot every Sunday'. So, even in the sixteenth century, it seems, chicken was a popular vote winner.

Today, chicken's versatility has made it a true staple in most of our homes, and good butchers will find you certified free-range, corn-fed or organic varieties that provide great flavour in your pot as well as peace of mind.

# Chicken

# Roast chicken with chestnut torn-bread stuffing

Considering this is such a classic, there are a whole lot of different ways to roast a chicken. Everyone seems to have their own 'trick': stuffing the bird with 40 cloves of garlic, roasting it upside down or basting every 7 minutes. Some like to cook it hot and fast for crispy skin, while others prefer a roast so slow the meat almost falls off the bone. I've included fast and slow instructions here, to cover all bases, and a really lovely modern take on chestnut stuffing (I love this so much, I don't bother stuffing the bird; I make a separate trayful).

1 x 1.6kg chicken, rinsed and dried
125ml dry white wine
500ml chicken stock
1 tablespoon tomato paste
1 tablespoon balsamic vinegar
20g cold butter (optional)

*to serve*
**chestnut torn-bread stuffing (right)**

Season the chicken with sea salt and black pepper inside and out and put, uncovered, on a plate in the fridge for up to 24 hours.

Preheat the oven to 240°C/gas mark 9 and also preheat your roasting tin at the same time. Put the chicken breast-side-up in the tin and roast for 20 minutes. Reduce the oven to 200°C/gas mark 6 and cook for another 30 minutes, or until the chicken juices run clear when you poke a skewer into the thigh.

Transfer the chicken to a plate and leave to rest in a warm place. Pour off the fat and put the tin over high heat on the stovetop. Pour in the wine and stock and stir well to scrape up the good crunchy bits from the tin. Add the tomato paste and vinegar and cook, stirring, until the gravy has reduced by half and thickened. If you like a richer gravy, whisk in the butter.

Serve with roast potatoes baked with rosemary. Your potatoes will take the same time as the chicken on another baking tray. Season with salt and pepper once cooked.
**Serves 4**

## Slow-roast chicken

Preheat the oven to 120°C/gas mark ½. Season the chicken inside and out, put breast-up in a roasting tin and roast for 2½ hours. Increase the heat to 220°C/gas mark 7 and cook for 30 minutes, or until the juices run clear.
**Serves 4**

## Chestnut torn-bread stuffing

1 loaf sourdough or other rustic bread, torn into small chunks
125ml olive oil
1 onion, finely chopped
1 fennel bulb, trimmed and finely chopped
2 garlic cloves, finely chopped
10 slices pancetta, chopped
200g cooked chestnuts, halved
300ml chicken stock
2 eggs, lightly beaten
leaves from 3 thyme sprigs

Preheat the oven to 200°C/gas mark 6. Put the bread in a large roasting tin and toss with all but 1 tablespoon of the olive oil. Bake for 15–20 minutes until crisp, then set aside.

Heat the remaining olive oil in a pan and fry the onion and fennel with a pinch of sea salt for 5 minutes until soft. Add the garlic and pancetta and fry until the pancetta turns golden. Add to the bread with the chestnuts, stock, eggs and thyme. Mix well and return to the oven for 30 minutes.
**Serves 4–6**

# Bill's coq au vin

Traditionally made with red wine and cooked overnight, classic coq au vin always seems to take forever and loses the thing I most love about chicken: the crispy skin. In this version you roast the chicken with lardons, then add white wine and finish off with freshly pan-fried mushrooms. That way you get both the lovely wine and herb-infused juices and the crispy chicken skin with non-flabby mushrooms.

1 x 1.5kg chicken, jointed
150g diced bacon or lardons
10 French shallots, peeled
a few thyme sprigs
a rosemary sprig
1 teaspoon dried chilli flakes
3 tablespoons olive oil
250ml white wine
a small knob of butter
350g mixed mushrooms (such as
    oyster and chestnut), sliced
3 garlic cloves, crushed with
    the back of a knife
a small handful of chopped
    flat-leaf parsley

*to serve*
crusty bread
green salad

Preheat the oven to 220°C/gas mark 7. Arrange the chicken pieces in a large roasting tin and scatter with the bacon, shallots, thyme, rosemary and chilli flakes. Season with sea salt and ground black pepper. Drizzle with 2 tablespoons of the olive oil and roast for 20 minutes.

Add the wine to the tin and roast for another 20–25 minutes. Remove from the oven.

Heat the butter and remaining oil in a large frying pan and cook the mushrooms and garlic over medium heat for 3–5 minutes. Tip into the tin and scatter with parsley. Serve with crusty bread and a green salad.

**Serves 4–6**

# Lemon chicken

More a modern Western invention than a traditional Chinese recipe, this has a retro appeal which is hard to resist when you fancy something sweet and sticky (as proven by my grandma). Restaurant versions that rely on cornflour can be a bit gluey — this recipe is lighter and more lemony. It's the ideal way to liven up a basic chicken breast; the gentle dusting with flour and five-spice powder makes the skin crispy and subtly aromatic.

2 tablespoons plain flour
1 teaspoon Chinese five-spice powder
100ml light-flavoured oil, such as
   sunflower, for shallow-frying
4 boneless chicken breasts,
   or suprèmes, with skin
1 lemon, cut into 8 wedges
3cm piece of fresh ginger,
   peeled and grated
80ml honey
80ml light soy sauce
juice of 2 lemons
2 tablespoons soft brown sugar

*to serve*
leaves from 1 small radicchio

Preheat the oven to 180°C/gas mark 4. Mix the flour and five-spice with sea salt and ground black pepper and toss the chicken in it until well coated.

Place your wok or large frying pan over medium–high heat. Add the oil and heat until hot. Add the chicken to the wok and fry for 3–5 minutes, until the skin is crispy. Drain on kitchen paper.

Put the chicken on a baking tray with the lemon wedges tucked in around the edges. Roast in the oven for 10 minutes, until the chicken is cooked through.

Meanwhile, drain all but 2 tablespoons of the oil from the wok and return to the heat. Add the ginger, honey, soy sauce, lemon juice and sugar and simmer for 2–3 minutes until thickened. Serve the chicken pieces whole or slice them, drizzle with the lemon glaze and serve with radicchio leaves.
**Serves 4**

# Chicken curry with lemon grass and ginger

I grew up on Keen's curry powder, an Australian classic. Even sausages could be curried at my house. I love Malaysian curries, but they can sometimes be a touch heavy on the coconut milk. This is another Bill hybrid — taking some of that Malaysian creaminess but making it a bit more brothlike, and adding a few Vietnamese notes for good measure.

**8 skinless chicken thighs, cut into quarters**
**2 tablespoons curry powder**
**1 tablespoon olive oil**
**4 red Asian shallots, sliced**
**1 red chilli, finely chopped (deseeded first, if you like)**
**1 lemon grass stalk, crushed with the back of a knife and split**
**5cm piece of fresh ginger, peeled and sliced**
**2 tablespoons fish sauce**
**1 tablespoon caster sugar**
**500g potatoes, peeled and cut into chunks**
**400ml chicken stock**
**250ml coconut milk**

*to serve*
**coriander leaves**
**rice vermicelli noodles or fluffy white baguette**

Put the chicken and curry powder in a bowl and toss to coat well. Season with sea salt.

Heat the oil in a large heavy-based pan over medium heat. Add the shallots and chilli and fry for 2 minutes. Add the chicken and cook until sealed and browned all over.

Add the lemon grass, ginger, fish sauce, sugar, potatoes and stock to the pan. Bring to the boil, cover and reduce the heat to medium–low. Simmer for 15–20 minutes.

Stir in the coconut milk, cover and simmer for another 5 minutes. Scatter with coriander leaves and serve with noodles or bread.
**Serves 4**

# 'Fried' chicken

This chicken, tenderised by buttermilk and gently spiced, crisply coated then baked, creates the same heavenly flavour contrasts as traditional Southern fried chicken. However, it comes with less oil and no mess, so you don't need to resurrect that deep-fat fryer that should've been sent to a car-boot sale years ago. Use fresh or flaky Japanese panko crumbs or plain white breadcrumbs. This is delicious with classic coleslaw or a simple salad of parsley and cucumber.

375ml buttermilk
  or low-fat yoghurt
1 teaspoon sea salt
1 teaspoon ground ginger
1 teaspoon turmeric
2 teaspoons ground coriander
2 teaspoons paprika
6 chicken drumsticks
6 chicken thighs
200g fresh white breadcrumbs

*to serve*
lime pickle
sliced cucumber
finely sliced red onion
flat-leaf parsley
lime wedges

Stir together the buttermilk, sea salt, ginger, turmeric, half the coriander and half the paprika in a large non-metallic bowl. Add the chicken, toss to coat well, and marinate in the fridge for up to 24 hours.

Preheat the oven to 190°C/gas mark 5. Remove the chicken from the fridge and brush a large baking tray with olive oil. Put the breadcrumbs in a large bowl and season with the remaining coriander and paprika, some sea salt and black pepper.

Working with one piece at a time, lift the chicken out of the marinade, coat evenly in the breadcrumbs and place on the tray. Bake in the oven for 40–45 minutes until golden brown and cooked through.

Serve with lime pickle and a simple salad of sliced cucumber, red onion and parsley leaves dressed with a squeeze of lime, sea salt and pepper.

**Serves 6**

'Fried chicken never harmed anyone (my wife likes to mention Elvis at this point), but I do balance it out with dark green leaves and tangy citrus.'

# Chicken burritos with coriander and green chilli

Burritos would have to be my fast food of choice. They beat the competition hands down — being fragrant, fresh and flavoursome, all in one easy-to-eat package. They also make ideal picnic food: take along all the fresh ingredients, nicely chopped and packed, then give everyone a flour tortilla and let them help themselves.

2 tablespoons olive oil
1 red onion, sliced
1–2 green chillies, finely chopped
   (deseeded first, if you like)
1 teaspoon ground coriander
1 teaspoon ground cumin
400g tin chopped tomatoes
1 teaspoon sugar
400g tin kidney beans, rinsed
4 flour tortillas
2 cooked chicken breasts, shredded
½ iceberg lettuce, shredded
a handful of coriander leaves
2 tomatoes, chopped
150g soured cream
1 avocado, sliced
lime juice, to taste

Heat the oil in a frying pan over medium heat. Add the onion and chilli and cook for 2–3 minutes, stirring frequently, until the onion is soft. Add the ground coriander and cumin and cook for 2 minutes. Add the tomatoes, sugar and beans and cook for 10 minutes.

Heat the tortillas under a hot grill or in a dry frying pan over medium heat.

To assemble, spoon the tomato mixture over the warm tortillas. Top with some chicken, lettuce, coriander leaves, tomato, soured cream and avocado slices. Season with sea salt and ground black pepper and finish with a squeeze of lime juice. Roll up the tortilla and serve immediately.

**Serves 4**

# Chicken Parmigiana

As a child my top-treat dinner was chicken schnitzel, topped with prosciutto and mozzarella and baked in tomato sauce. My metabolism isn't quite what it was or I would still eat this on a regular basis (the girls have to restrain me). This is my modern take on a childhood classic that never fails to bring back memories of a time when I didn't have to worry about my waistline.

2 tablespoons olive oil,
   plus extra for drizzling
2 garlic cloves, crushed
400g tin chopped tomatoes
1 teaspoon sea salt
1 teaspoon sugar
a handful of torn basil leaves
4 chicken breasts
100g fresh mozzarella
   cheese, roughly torn
50g grated Parmesan

*to serve*
green salad
crusty bread

Heat half the olive oil in a saucepan, add the garlic and cook, stirring, for a few seconds. Add the tomatoes, salt, sugar and some ground black pepper and cook, stirring occasionally, for about 15 minutes until the oil rises to the surface and the sauce reduces and thickens. Remove from the heat and stir in the basil.

Preheat the oven to 180°C/gas mark 4. Heat the remaining oil in a large non-stick frying pan over high heat. Add the chicken, cook for 1–2 minutes each side until golden and then transfer to a large baking dish.

Pour the tomato sauce over the chicken, top with the mozzarella and sprinkle with Parmesan. Drizzle with a little more olive oil.

Bake for 20 minutes until the cheese is melted and bubbling. Serve with green salad and crusty bread.

**Serves 4**

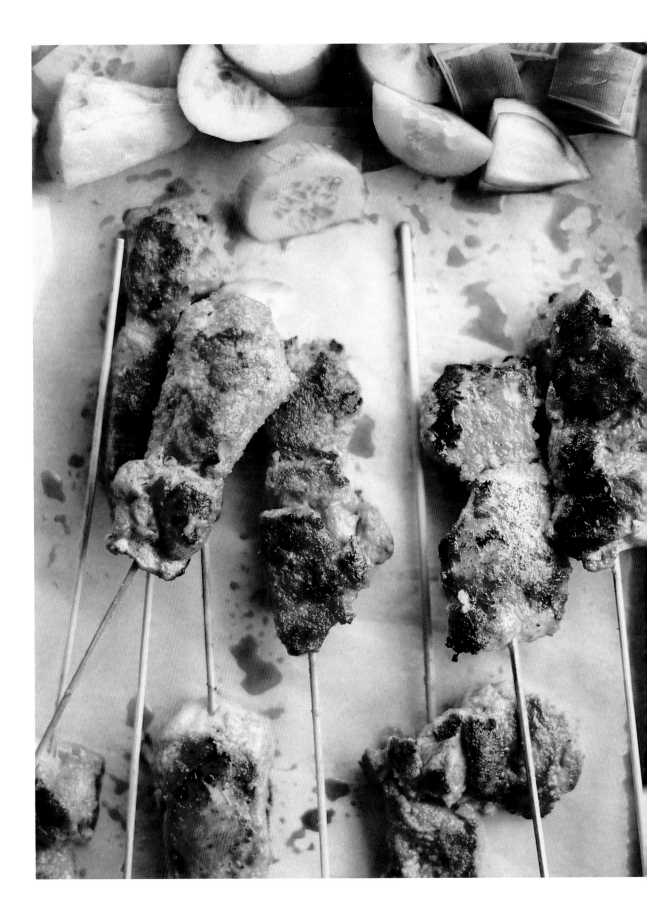

# Chicken satay

Satay skewers are one of my favourite street foods, but I can't always be bothered to thread the chicken onto skewers at home. You can use this marinade on chicken thighs, wings, legs or even strips of breast, threaded onto skewers or not, depending on how your day is panning out. I serve this with a pile of fresh pineapple, cucumber and red onion to make a sweet, crunchy, cooling contrast.

**1 lemon grass stalk, crushed
  with the back of a knife
  and roughly chopped
3 garlic cloves, roughly chopped
3cm piece of fresh ginger, peeled
  and roughly chopped
1 tablespoon sugar
1 teaspoon sea salt
1 teaspoon turmeric
50g peanuts
4 skinless chicken thighs,
  halved lengthways**

*to serve*
**satay sauce (right)
fresh pineapple, cut into chunks
red onion, cut into chunks
cucumber, cut into chunks**

Whiz the lemon grass, garlic, ginger, sugar, salt, turmeric, peanuts and 125ml water in a blender or food processor until smooth. Transfer to a large bowl, add the chicken and toss well to coat. Cover and leave to marinate in a cool place for at least 1 hour.

If you're using skewers, preheat the grill to high (if you're using wooden skewers, soak in water beforehand to prevent scorching). Thread the chicken onto 8 skewers and grill for 5–8 minutes on each side.

If you're not using skewers, barbecue or pan-fry the chicken in a non-stick frying pan over medium–high heat for 5–8 minutes on each side. Serve with satay sauce and chunks of pineapple, onion and cucumber.
**Serves 4**

## Satay sauce

250ml coconut cream
1 tablespoon red curry paste
100g coarsely ground
  dry-roasted peanuts
1 tablespoon soft brown sugar
2 tablespoons soy sauce
1 tablespoon lime juice

Heat half the coconut cream in a saucepan over medium heat until just simmering. Stir in the curry paste until smooth and fragrant. Add the peanuts, sugar, soy sauce, lime juice and the rest of the coconut cream and stir for 5 minutes until thickened.
**Serves 4**

# Chicken and dried apricot pilaf

When I was growing up, dinner would sometimes be one of those rehydrated packets of 'flavoured rice'. So, it was a quite extraordinary experience when I first made a beautiful simple pilaf — rich with spices, dried fruit, nuts and the flavours of honey, ginger and orange zest — and suddenly realised what was supposed to have been in those packets.

2 tablespoons olive oil
8 chicken thighs
1 onion, chopped
2 garlic cloves, crushed
4cm piece of fresh ginger,
    peeled and grated
3 teaspoons ras el hanout
400g basmati rice
750ml chicken stock
1 teaspoon honey
zest of 1 orange
1 tablespoon sherry vinegar
100g chopped pistachios
200g chopped dried apricots
2 handfuls of fresh coriander

*to serve*
date relish (right)
broad bean and pomegranate
    salad (right)
yoghurt

Heat the oil in a large pan (I use a deep cast-iron frying pan), sear the chicken for 1–2 minutes on each side and remove from the pan.

Add a bit more oil if needed and cook the onion, stirring occasionally, with a pinch of sea salt until soft and translucent. Add the garlic and ginger and cook for 1–2 minutes. Add the ras el hanout and cook until fragrant. Stir in the rice, return the chicken to the pan and pour in the stock. Stir in the honey, orange zest and sherry vinegar.

Bring to the boil, cover the pan, turn down to a simmer and cook for about 40 minutes until the stock has been absorbed and the rice is cooked. Stir in the pistachios, dried apricots and coriander.

Serve with date relish, broad bean and pomegranate salad and yoghurt on the side.
**Serves 4**

## Date relish

Chop and remove pits from 200g dried medjool dates. Mix with the juice of 1 lemon, 2 tablespoons chopped flat-leaf parsley and 2–3 tablespoons extra-virgin olive oil. Season with sea salt and ground black pepper.
**Serves 4**

## Broad bean and pomegranate salad

Blanch 200g shelled broad beans and refresh in cold water. Gently stir the broad beans with the seeds of ½ pomegranate, the juice of ½ orange, 1 teaspoon sherry vinegar and 2–3 tablespoons extra-virgin olive oil. Season with sea salt and ground black pepper and scatter with coriander leaves.
**Serves 4**

# Piri piri poussin

There used to be one of those piri piri chicken places down the road from us in Bondi many years ago. Now it's a brand and one of the most popular fast foods in the world. There's something very moreish about strongly marinated chicken, burning with chilli heat and almost over-grilled so that it falls off the bone.

My version of this virtually no-cook sauce is foolproof. Your butcher will 'spatchcock' a poussin or small chicken by removing the backbone and flattening the bird.

**250ml olive oil, plus extra for frying**
**2 green chillies, roughly chopped**
**2 red chillies, roughly chopped**
**1 teaspoon dried chilli flakes**
**1 teaspoon sea salt**
**4 garlic cloves, roughly chopped**
**1 tablespoon lemon juice**
**2 x 500g poussins (small chickens),**
**backbones removed and flattened**

Whiz the oil, chillies and flakes, salt, garlic and lemon juice in a blender until smooth. Transfer to a pan over medium heat and warm through for 5 minutes. Slash the poussins in a few places on each side.

Put the poussins in a shallow bowl and rub all over with the warm marinade. Cover with cling film and marinate in the fridge for at least 30 minutes.

Heat a covered barbecue to high. Place the poussins, skin-down, on the rack, close the lid and cook for 15–20 minutes, or until cooked through (alternatively, cook, skin-up, in a 220°C/gas mark 7 oven for 15–20 minutes). Baste during cooking for extra piri piri intensity.

The piri piri sauce can be stored in a jar in the fridge for up to a week and used to marinate chicken, pork or fish.
**Serves 4**

Since I came from a family of butchers, while other kids were obsessed with football or boxing, all my school projects were about meat. Dad even gave me cow anatomy posters to take into school, so I could tell the rest of the class where the cuts came from. I'm sure they all still remember that particular show-and-tell!

These days we're gaining far more respect for the meat we eat. We know that it's healthier for us to eat less, so we want the meat we do eat to be better quality. Another current trend I love is the slow-cooking revival. Braising, slow-roasting and simmering all make a lot of sense to me in this hectic world we inhabit.

Everyone should know how to cook a perfect steak, or roast beef and gravy — some of the great classic meat dishes just can't be improved upon. But while sweet and sour pork was always my favourite Chinese meal as a child, when I tasted it again recently I found I'd outgrown the flavours. So I've been working on an updated, rather less cloying, version with basil and chunks of fresh pineapple.

I was also surprised to find I prefer my beef daube made with a light summer rosé rather than the traditional red wine. And crisp and succulent pork belly broken up over bitter greens with slices of ripe pear is my new take on the traditional Sunday lunch.

# Meat

# Crisp pork belly with apple sauce

Who doesn't love pork crackling? (Sorry, vegetarians!) This has become a very fashionable dish in restaurants, with the slow cooking producing the most wonderfully succulent meat under that crunchy skin and melting crackling layer. I like this as a classic Sunday lunch with apple sauce, roast spuds and a salad of bitter leaves like chicory and radicchio with a mustard dressing. Or break up the crisp pork belly over the bitter leaves and add thin slices of apple or pear for a lighter meal.

**900g pork belly**
**sea salt**
**3 bay leaves**
**4 garlic cloves, squashed with**
**    the back of a knife**
**3 strips of orange peel**

*to serve*
**apple sauce (right)**
**bitter salad leaves**

Preheat the oven to 140°C/gas mark 1 and score the pork belly lengthways with a sharp knife (a craft knife is useful for this). Rub the pork belly with lots of sea salt, making sure you get into the score marks. Put, uncovered, in the fridge for 30 minutes to dry out.

Put the bay leaves, garlic and orange peel in a roasting tin and place the pork belly on top. Pour 1cm cold water into the tin and roast the pork, uncovered, for 3 hours.

Increase the oven to 220°C/gas mark 8 and roast the pork for 20–30 minutes, or until the skin crackles. (If the skin won't crackle, put under a hot grill for 1–2 minutes.) Remove from the oven, cover with foil and leave to rest for 15 minutes. Serve with apple sauce and salad leaves.
**Serves 4–6**

## Apple sauce

Peel, core and cut 4 apples into quarters. Put in a saucepan with 60ml water. Cover the pan and simmer over medium heat for 10 minutes until the apple is soft.

Add 2 tablespoons caster sugar, a knob of butter, 1 tablespoon lemon juice and a pinch of mixed spice. Stir until the sugar has dissolved and the butter melted, then remove from the heat and cool a little before serving.
**Serves 4–6**

# Chinese-style marinated pork

This is a variation on the barbecued pork char siu you see hanging in the windows of Chinatown restaurants, unfortunately often varnished with red food colouring and maltose. I prefer to spice up my pork with aromatics and a combination of sweet and savoury sauces. So, more a flavour hit than a colour hit. This marinade is also delicious on pork chops for a weeknight dinner.

2 tablespoons hoisin sauce
2 tablespoons honey
1 teaspoon sesame oil
2 tablespoons soy sauce
½ teaspoon Chinese five-spice powder
3 garlic cloves, crushed
1 tablespoon soft brown sugar
1 x 400g pork fillet

*to serve*
seasonal greens with
   oyster sauce (right)
steamed rice
red chilli, finely sliced
crisp-fried red Asian shallots
   (I use store-bought)

Put the hoisin sauce, honey, sesame oil, soy sauce, five-spice, garlic, sugar and some ground black pepper in a small pan and heat for 5 minutes. Allow to cool, then rub two-thirds of the mixture into the pork. Put in a non-metallic bowl, cover and marinate for at least 2 hours, or overnight if possible. Keep the remaining marinade.

Preheat the oven to 220°C/gas mark 7. Put the pork in a roasting tin and roast for 15–20 minutes, brushing regularly with the remaining marinade. Leave to rest for 10 minutes before slicing and serving with seasonal greens, rice, chilli and crisp-fried Asian shallots.
**Serves 4**

### Seasonal greens with oyster sauce

Blanch 1 bunch of Chinese greens in a little water containing a teaspoon of light-flavoured oil, such as sunflower. Mix together 2 tablespoons oyster sauce, 1 tablespoon water, another ½ teaspoon of oil, ½ teaspoon sugar and a pinch of pepper. Drizzle over the drained vegetables.
**Serves 4**

# Lamb shank tagine with apricots

When I was growing up in the Melbourne suburbs there was a favourite dish called apricot chicken. It was basically that — chicken baked with tinned apricots — and almost succeeded in putting me off the idea of meat cooked with fruit for life. Thankfully, this Moroccan classic persuaded me to give the combination another try. You don't need a special tagine dish: it's deliciously unlike apricot chicken, whatever you cook it in.

1 tablespoon ground cinnamon
1 teaspoon ground coriander
1 teaspoon turmeric
1 teaspoon ground cumin
1.6kg lamb shanks
1 tablespoon light-flavoured
   oil, such as sunflower
1 onion, grated
1 tablespoon grated fresh ginger
1 preserved lemon, rinsed, flesh
   removed and chopped
600g orange sweet potatoes,
   peeled and chopped
250ml chicken stock
a handful of dried apricots
2 tablespoons honey
lemon juice

*to serve*
coriander leaves
steamed couscous
carrot and coriander salad (right)

Preheat the oven to 170°C/gas mark 3. Mix together the cinnamon, coriander, turmeric and cumin and rub over the lamb.

Heat the oil in a large flameproof casserole dish over medium–high heat on the stovetop. Sear the lamb shanks until browned all over and then add the onion, ginger, preserved lemon, sweet potatoes, stock and apricots. Season with sea salt and ground black pepper.

Bring to the boil, put a tight-fitting lid on the dish and put in the oven for 2 hours, or until the meat is tender and falling off the bone.

Remove the dish from the oven and place over medium–high heat on the stovetop. Stir in the honey and lemon juice to taste. Cook for 10–15 minutes until the sauce has thickened.

Garnish with coriander leaves and serve with steamed couscous and carrot and coriander salad.
**Serves 4–6**

## Carrot and coriander salad

Grate 3 carrots and mix together with a handful of black olives, a large handful of chopped fresh coriander, 2 tablespoons extra-virgin olive oil and 2 tablespoons lemon juice. Season to taste with sea salt and ground black pepper.
**Serves 4–6**

# 'Sweet and sour' pork with pineapple and basil

Sweet and sour pork was always my childhood favourite when we ate our weekly dinner in the local Chinese restaurant. This universal dish is one I've eaten in London, Rome and even Varanasi. My version uses the same combination of flavours, but without the cloying sweetness, or the batter!

600g lean pork fillets, thinly sliced
2 tablespoons yellow curry paste
2 tablespoons light-flavoured
    oil, such as sunflower
200g chopped fresh pineapple
1 red onion, cut into thin wedges
250g green beans, topped
250g cherry tomatoes, halved
2 tablespoons lime juice
1 tablespoon fish sauce
1 tablespoon soft brown sugar
a large handful of basil leaves

*to serve*
steamed rice

Put the pork in a bowl with the curry paste and stir well until it is evenly coated.

Place a wok over high heat. Add half the oil and heat until hot. Add the pork in batches and stir-fry for 2–3 minutes until golden and cooked through, then remove from the wok. Stir-fry the pineapple for 1 minute to caramelise, then remove from the wok.

Reheat the wok to high and add the remaining oil. Add the onion and stir-fry for 2 minutes until golden. Add the beans and 2 tablespoons water to the wok and stir-fry for 1–2 minutes. Add the tomatoes and stir-fry for 1 minute.

Return the pork and pineapple to the wok, toss together well, then add the lime juice, fish sauce, sugar and basil leaves and give a final stir. Serve immediately with rice.

**Serves 4**

# Perfect steak

What is there to say about perfectly cooked steak? That it reminds us that simple things are sometimes the best? Cooking a great steak is a bit like knowing your eight-times table or how to change a flat tyre — general knowledge everyone should have. Here's how to cook your steak, and a choice of sauces to serve it with.

**4 x 250g sirloin steaks, each
  about 2.5cm thick
2 tablespoons olive oil**

Let the steaks come to room temperature before you cook them. Brush them with olive oil and season well with sea salt and ground black pepper.

Heat a large frying pan over high heat for a few minutes. Sear the steaks for 2 minutes on each side for rare; 3–4 minutes on each side for medium; and 4–5 minutes on each side for well done. Serve with one of these sauces, or horseradish cream (page 81).

**Serves 4**

## Green peppercorn sauce

1 garlic clove, crushed
1 heaped tablespoon green
  peppercorns in brine, drained
2 tablespoons brandy
150ml beef stock
150ml double cream
2 teaspoons Dijon mustard

When you take your steak out of the pan, put the pan back over medium heat and cook the garlic and peppercorns for about 30 seconds. Add the brandy and allow to sizzle. Add the stock and simmer for a minute or two until just reduced. Add the cream and mustard and stir for 2 minutes until thickened and glossy.

**Serves 4**

## Bearnaise sauce

Stir 1 tablespoon chopped tarragon and 1 tablespoon chopped chervil into 1 quantity hollandaise sauce (page 18). Heat gently.

**Serves 4**

'Making great-tasting gravy from the meat juices in your roasting tin is simple work. Pour off the excess fat, shake in a bit of flour and stir over heat (making sure to scrape up any crunchy bits that are stuck to the tin). Add stock and stir until thickened. A spoonful of soy sauce works wonders, too.'

# Beef daube with rosé

I love a wintery beef stew made with robust red wine, but I decided to try this with rosé last summer when I had a bottle of the pink stuff left over from a party. I was amazed at how well it turned out: light and zingy and lifted by the orange zest. And you don't even need to sear the meat: just throw everything in together and then serve with buttered noodles dressed in the sauce.

2 tablespoons plain flour
1.5kg beef, cut into 2.5cm cubes
80ml olive oil
1 large red onion, sliced
6 garlic cloves, crushed with
   the back of a knife
400g tin chopped tomatoes
3 carrots, peeled and cut into chunks
a couple of thyme sprigs
1 bay leaf
peel from 1 orange, cut into strips
500ml rosé wine
500ml beef stock
6 anchovy fillets, chopped (optional)
100g pitted black olives (optional)

*to serve*
500g tagliatelle
300g spinach
30g butter

Preheat the oven to 160°C/gas mark 3. Season the flour with sea salt and black pepper and use to coat the beef. Put the beef and the remaining ingredients in a large flameproof casserole dish and bring to the boil on the stovetop. Season with sea salt and pepper. Cover the surface of the stew with a piece of crumpled baking paper and then a tight-fitting lid. Bake for 3 hours, or until the meat is meltingly tender.

Remove the stew from the oven, take off the lid and leave while you cook the pasta in boiling salted water until al dente. Drain and return the pasta to its pan, stir in the spinach, butter and 2 ladlefuls of broth from the stew. Season with sea salt and black pepper and serve with the stew.

**Serves 6**

# Roast lamb shoulder

You simply can't be Australian and not love roast lamb. A leg is the traditional joint to roast, but it can be expensive. I find shoulder much tastier, and these days I prefer my lamb cooked slowly so it's fall-off-the-bone tender, rather than struggling to get it perfectly pink but not completely raw in the middle. I jazz up my mint sauce with parsley and garlic for a bit more body.

1 x 1.1kg lamb shoulder with bone
2 tablespoons olive oil
1 whole garlic bulb, halved
3 rosemary sprigs

*to serve*
potatoes, roasted with oregano
mint sauce (right)
my Greek salad (right)

Preheat the oven to 160°C/gas mark 3. Trim the lamb of any excess fat, rub with the oil and season with sea salt and pepper. Put the garlic and lamb in a roasting tin and scatter with rosemary. Add 250ml water, cover with foil and roast for 2 hours.

Uncover the lamb, increase the oven to 220°C/gas mark 7 and roast for another 20 minutes to brown. The meat should be tender and falling off the bone.
**Serves 4**

## Barbecued lamb shoulder

You can also cook the lamb on the barbecue, but you need a boneless shoulder for this version. Preheat a covered barbecue to medium–high. Place the lamb, skin-down, on the rack and turn the barbecue to low. Close the lid and cook for 10 minutes. Turn over and cook for 20 minutes, or until cooked medium-rare. Leave to rest in a warm place for 10 minutes before serving.
**Serves 4**

## Mint sauce

1 garlic clove, crushed
a large handful of flat-leaf
    parsley, finely chopped
a large handful of mint, finely chopped
2 tablespoons white wine vinegar
2 teaspoons extra-virgin olive oil
1 teaspoon sugar
a pinch of chilli flakes

Stir together all the ingredients and season with a pinch of sea salt.
**Serves 4**

## My Greek salad

2 small Lebanese cucumbers, chopped
1 small red onion, finely sliced
1 red or green pepper, chopped
100g feta cheese, crumbled
a large handful of flat-leaf parsley leaves
2 tablespoons extra-virgin olive oil
juice of 1 lemon
a handful of green olives, pitted
    if you have the time

Toss together all the ingredients and season with sea salt and black pepper.
**Serves 4**

# Roast beef fillet with red wine glaze

This is an overtly extravagant cut of meat, but sometimes it's just what's needed, especially if there's a cause for celebration. The trick is not to cook it for too long — roast beef really should be rare, so, if you prefer yours medium-to-well done, buy a fattier cut. The crème fraîche mash and maybe some sautéed spinach are all you need for a simple yet supremely elegant supper.

1 x 1.5kg beef fillet
2 tablespoons olive oil

*red wine glaze*
1 French shallot, finely chopped
100ml red wine
250ml beef stock
1 tablespoon balsamic vinegar

*to serve*
crème fraîche mash (right)

Preheat the oven to 240°C/gas mark 9. Brush the beef with the oil and season with sea salt and pepper. Heat a large frying pan over high heat. When very hot, sear the beef on all sides until browned, then put into a roasting tin.

Roast the beef for 20–25 minutes for rare (7 minutes per 500g) and 30 minutes for medium (10 minutes per 500g). Lift the beef onto a board, cover loosely with foil and leave to rest for 5–10 minutes.

While the beef is resting, make the red wine glaze. Put the roasting tin over low heat on the stovetop and add the shallot. Cook, stirring, for a few minutes. Increase the heat and add the red wine and stock, scraping the bottom of the tin to mix in the crunchy bits. Cook for 6–8 minutes, or until reduced by half. Stir in the balsamic vinegar, then strain and serve with the beef.

**Serves 4–6**

## Crème fraîche mash

800g potatoes,
    peeled and chopped
150ml milk
25g butter
100ml crème fraîche or single cream

Cook the potatoes in boiling water until tender. Remove from the heat, drain well and return to the hot pan. Mash the potatoes (for special occasions I like to blend them until smooth in a mixer with a paddle attachment).

Heat the milk and butter in a small pan over medium heat (don't allow to boil) until the butter has melted. Beat into the potatoes and then fold in the crème fraîche or cream. Season with sea salt.

**Serves 4–6**

# Lamb curry with yoghurt and tomatoes

While the ingredient list might look long, these are mostly easy-to-find spices that you probably already have in your store cupboard. The dish needs a good couple of hours' cooking, but there's something quite restful, I find, about letting it simmer away on the stovetop while you read the paper or have a long, leisurely bath. This is traditionally quite dry but you can add more liquid if you prefer it saucier.

1kg lamb leg, cut into 5cm cubes
2 teaspoons ground coriander
1 teaspoon ground cumin
1 teaspoon turmeric
1 teaspoon dried chilli flakes
1 teaspoon paprika
1 teaspoon cardamom pods, crushed
3 cinnamon sticks
1 tablespoon finely grated fresh ginger
1 tablespoon olive oil
25g butter
2 large onions, chopped
400g tin chopped tomatoes
250g yoghurt
juice of 1 lime
2 teaspoons sugar

*to serve*
steamed rice
chutney

Put the lamb in a large bowl, add the spices and ginger and toss to coat well. Season with sea salt.

Place a large heavy-based pan over medium–high heat. Heat the oil and butter and cook the onion for 5 minutes until soft. Add the spiced lamb and cook for 5 minutes until browned.

Add the tomatoes, yoghurt and 250ml water to the pan and bring to the boil. Turn the heat down to medium–low, cover the pan and simmer for 2 hours. Stir in the lime juice and sugar and serve with steamed rice and your favourite chutney.

**Serves 6**

# Crumbed veal cutlets

Every country seems to have its own version of the schnitzel — so much so that the restaurant world has a saying: 'If you want to sell it, crumb it!' Japan has tonkatsu, made from pork and served with bulldog sauce (a bit like HP only better). I like my crumbed cutlets with roasted peppers and a fresh tomato salad, or perhaps broccoli with chilli and garlic.

4 x 220g veal cutlets
150g plain flour
60ml milk
2 eggs, lightly beaten
160g fresh white breadcrumbs
a small handful of flat-leaf
    parsley, chopped
1 teaspoon sea salt
3 tablespoons olive oil
60g butter

*to serve*
**peppers and oregano (right)**

Flatten the veal cutlets to about 1cm thick with a meat mallet. Put the flour in a bowl and season with sea salt and pepper. Whisk the milk and eggs in a separate bowl. Mix together the breadcrumbs, parsley and sea salt in another bowl.

Dip each cutlet in the flour to coat. Shake off the excess, then coat in the egg and finally coat in a layer of the breadcrumbs.

Heat the olive oil and butter in a large non-stick frying pan over medium heat. Cook the cutlets in batches (it's important not to overcrowd the pan) for 2–3 minutes on one side until crisp and golden, then turn over and cook for 2 minutes on the other side. Place on kitchen paper in a warm oven while you cook the rest. Serve with peppers and oregano.
**Serves 4**

## Peppers and oregano

2 large red peppers
2 large yellow peppers
2 tablespoons extra-virgin olive oil
2 tablespoons red wine vinegar
1 garlic clove, very thinly sliced
1 tablespoon oregano leaves

Preheat the oven to 180°C/gas mark 4. Put the red and yellow peppers on a large baking tray and roast for 25 minutes, or until slightly blackened and wilted. Transfer to a large bowl, cover with cling film and leave for 20 minutes to loosen the skins.

Peel the peppers and remove the seeds, then roughly tear and mix with the olive oil, red wine vinegar, garlic and oregano leaves. Season with sea salt and black pepper before serving.
**Serves 4**

## Oven-baked cutlets

Preheat the oven to 220°C/gas mark 7. Arrange the crumbed cutlets in a single layer on a baking tray. Brush with melted butter and bake for 6–8 minutes until golden. Turn and bake for another 5 minutes until golden.
**Serves 4**

Apart from the odd bag of prawns from the seafood van outside Dad's shop (he'd swap them for a steak), I didn't eat much seafood until I moved to Sydney. Looking back now, I don't know how I survived without salt and pepper squid, crisp-skinned salmon and steamed white fish. These are the basics I turn to when I need a good physical and psychological dose of omega 3.

Fish is nature's fast food. The best fish, as long as it's as fresh as you can possibly get it, often doesn't need anything more than a flash in a pan, a sprinkle of sea salt and a squeeze of lemon. Sometimes I rev it up with Asian flavours for a bit more bite, or whip up a quick sidekick such as green goddess dressing, raita or tartare sauce.

In winter, when I crave a warm kitchen and a heartier dinner, I still turn to seafood. Then I make a filo-topped pie, fish cakes to use up leftover mash, or perhaps a pot of mussels in white wine. And I can't help spicing up my versions a touch, with chilli in my fish cakes and in the dressing for my steamed fish.

# Seafood

# Pan-fried fish with two sauces

In his bachelor days a friend of mine made fish with asparagus and beurre blanc as his signature dish… the signature part being that he cooked it in his dishwasher. We would all arrive for dinner and hear that familiar mechanical whir! Today I prefer my fish cooked on a conventional stovetop. The trick to perfect pan-frying is to turn the fish only once — it should be crisp outside and soft and melting within. The beurre blanc is a classic; the lemon salsa, a little more modern and zingy.

4 x 200g firm white fish fillets,
   with skin or without
1 tablespoon olive oil

*to serve*
**beurre blanc or lemon salsa (right)**

Heat a frying pan over medium–high heat for 2 minutes. Brush the fish with oil and season well with sea salt and ground black pepper. Cook the fish, skin-down if your fish has skin, for 3 minutes. Turn the fish over and cook for 1 minute until golden and just cooked through. Serve with beurre blanc or lemon salsa.

**Serves 4**

## Beurre blanc

4 small French shallots, roughly chopped
100ml white wine
250g butter, chilled and diced

Put the shallots in a small saucepan over medium heat. Add the wine, turn the heat to high and simmer rapidly until the wine has reduced by half. Turn the heat down to low.

Gradually whisk in the cold butter, a cube at a time, until it has all been added and the sauce is thick and glossy. Strain through a fine sieve and season with salt and pepper.

**Serves 4**

## Lemon salsa

Segment a lemon by first slicing off both ends. Stand the fruit on a board and, following the curve of the lemon, slice off the peel and pith with a very sharp knife. Cut out the segments by slicing between the membranes. Put the segments in a bowl (and add any juice). Stir in a handful of flat-leaf parsley leaves, 8–10 torn green olives, 2 tablespoons extra-virgin olive oil, 1 tablespoon capers, 2 finely sliced spring onions and plenty of sea salt.

**Serves 4**

# Gravlax

People think curing fish must be complicated, but it couldn't be easier: the fridge does all the work and you take all the credit. This makes a nice Scandinavian change to smoked salmon and is an impressive dish to serve to a big group of friends, especially at Christmas.

3 teaspoons coriander seeds
2 teaspoons white peppercorns
2 teaspoons black peppercorns
3 tablespoons sea salt
1 tablespoon caster sugar
800g side of salmon, with skin,
    trimmed if required
a large bunch of dill, roughly chopped

*to serve*
mustard dill dressing (right)
rye bread

Dry-toast the coriander and peppercorns in a frying pan over medium heat until fragrant. Transfer to a mortar and pestle and grind to a powder. Stir in the salt and sugar.

Put the salmon fillet, skin-up, in a wide shallow dish. Scatter evenly with a third of the spice mix. Press a third of the chopped dill onto the skin. Turn the fish over and scatter with the rest of the spice mix and then the rest of the dill. Cover the fish tightly with cling film and weigh down with a baking tray and a couple of heavy tins. Put in the fridge for 2–3 days, turning every 12 hours or so.

Unwrap the dish and brush the dill off the salmon. Place the salmon fillet, skin-down, on a chopping board and, with a long sharp knife, carefully carve very thin diagonal slivers of pink flesh off the salmon. Serve with mustard dill dressing and rye bread.

**Serves 10**

## Mustard dill dressing

1 tablespoon Dijon mustard
1 tablespoon caster sugar
1 teaspoon sea salt
2 tablespoons white wine vinegar
125ml light-flavoured oil, such as sunflower
2 tablespoons chopped dill

Whisk the mustard, sugar, salt and vinegar until the sugar has dissolved, then whisk in the oil in a thin stream. Stir in the dill.

**Dresses 1 side of salmon**

# Baked whole fish with roasted tomato and pineapple relish

Sharing a fish with friends is something that feels as old as time — updated here for the twenty-first century by a marinade of Asian flavours and a fruity relish. This is entirely simple to make, yet has a real 'wow' factor.

1 large snapper (about 1kg)
3 tablespoons light-flavoured
  oil, such as sunflower
2 tablespoons soy sauce
2 tablespoons grated fresh ginger
1 tablespoon finely chopped garlic
2 tablespoons sugar
2 teaspoons turmeric
2 teaspoons sea salt

*to serve*
**roasted tomato and pineapple
  relish (right)**

Give the snapper a good rinse and leave the head on. Score the fish skin on both sides in a crisscross pattern with a sharp knife. Put on a baking tray lined with baking paper.

Stir together the oil, soy sauce, ginger, garlic, sugar, turmeric and salt. Pour over the snapper and massage into the scores on the skin. Cover and refrigerate for at least 20 minutes, then remove from the fridge 10 minutes before cooking. Preheat the oven to 200°C/gas mark 6.

Bake the fish for 30–35 minutes. Serve with roasted tomato and pineapple relish.
**Serves 4–6**

## Roasted tomato and pineapple relish

4 ripe tomatoes, quartered
  lengthways, seeds removed
1 long red chilli, chopped
  (deseeded first, if you like)
200g fresh pineapple pieces
1 tablespoon light-flavoured
  oil, such as sunflower
2 tablespoons soft brown sugar
2 tablespoons lime juice
2 tablespoons fish sauce
8–10 Thai basil or sweet basil
  leaves, torn (optional)

Preheat the oven to 200°C/gas mark 6. Toss the tomatoes, chilli and pineapple in the oil. Arrange on a baking tray and roast for 15–20 minutes until golden. Leave until cool enough to handle. Peel the skin off the tomatoes and chilli.

Put the tomatoes, chilli and pineapple in a bowl, add the brown sugar, lime juice, fish sauce and basil and toss together gently.
**Serves 4–6**

# Fish pie

Some people like their fish pie with a classic béchamel sauce and mashed potato topping. I enjoy mine made with a mixture of different fish and a crisp filo pastry top. Filo doesn't need long in the oven and doesn't like sitting around afterwards, so bring this pie straight to the table and serve with a simple green salad and some very cold white wine.

2 tablespoons olive oil
25g butter
4 leeks, white part only, thinly sliced
3 garlic cloves, crushed
1 tablespoon grated fresh ginger
800g mixed fish, such as firm white fish and salmon, cut into chunks
2 tablespoons chopped dill
80g melted butter, plus extra for greasing
8 sheets filo pastry, plus a few extra just in case

*soured cream relish*
300g soured cream
1 tablespoon snipped chives
2 spring onions, sliced
1 tablespoon lime juice

Heat the olive oil and butter in a 28cm non-stick ovenproof frying pan over medium–low heat. Add the leek, garlic and ginger and cook, stirring occasionally, for 8–10 minutes until the leek is soft. Stir in the fish pieces and dill and season with sea salt and ground black pepper. Remove from the frying pan and wipe out the pan.

Preheat the oven to 200°C/gas mark 6. Lightly grease the cleaned pan with melted butter. Place the filo sheets on a clean work surface, cover with a damp tea towel and work with one sheet at a time. Line the pan with a sheet of pastry, letting the pastry edges hang over the side of the pan. Brush the pastry with melted butter and place another filo sheet on top, brushing that one with butter, too. Lay the sheets at different angles so they fan out around the edge of the pan. Continue until you have used all 8 sheets, brushing with butter as you go.

Spoon the fish filling into the pan and fold the overhanging pastry edges over the filling to cover it. (If they don't cover it completely, trim a few extra sheets of filo to top the pie.) Bake for 15–20 minutes, then carefully hold a baking tray over the pan and turn over so the pie turns out onto the tray. Return to the oven for 15–20 minutes until golden.

Meanwhile, make the relish by stirring together all the ingredients and seasoning with sea salt and ground black pepper. Serve with the fish pie.

**Serves 4**

# Fish cakes

What a modern classic the humble fish cake has become. Yet, while we've come to expect it in restaurants, to me it almost feels a shame to use fresh fish for making these at home. For this everyday version I use good-quality tinned salmon and pep it up with lots of spring onions, parsley and lemon zest. This is definitely my favourite way to use up leftover mash.

300g potatoes, peeled and chopped
   (or leftover mash, page 173)
415g tin red salmon, drained
40g plain flour, plus extra for dusting
2 eggs
4 spring onions, chopped
3 tablespoons chopped flat-leaf parsley
3 tablespoons chopped coriander
1 large green chilli, finely chopped
   (deseeded first, if you like)
1 teaspoon grated fresh ginger
2 tablespoons crème fraîche
160g fresh breadcrumbs
zest of 1 lemon
light-flavoured oil, such as
   sunflower, for shallow-frying

*to serve*
**raita (right)**
**lemon or lime wedges**

Boil the potatoes in salted water for about 25 minutes until tender. Drain and roughly mash. Put in a bowl with the salmon, flour, eggs, spring onions, parsley, coriander, chilli, ginger, crème fraîche, breadcrumbs and lemon zest and season with sea salt and pepper. Mix well and shape into 12 patties, then dust with a little flour.

Heat the oil in a frying pan over medium–high heat. Fry the fish cakes in batches for 2–3 minutes on each side until golden. Serve with raita and lemon wedges.
**Serves 4**

## Raita

250g yoghurt
1 Lebanese cucumber, peeled,
   seeded and finely chopped
1 tablespoon chopped mint

Stir together all the ingredients and season with sea salt and ground black pepper.
**Serves 4**

'Make sure your mussels are healthy and firmly closed (a tap on the bench should make them clam up), then pull off any clinging beards. For a speedy supper, cook mussels with crushed garlic and a little white wine in a large pan with a lid. They take only a few minutes to open.'

# Crisp-skinned salmon salad with green goddess dressing

When I first tasted this dressing in the States I knew I had to make it because I loved the name so much. It's an excellent way to make a creamy dressing that's not too heavy, and it goes perfectly with the oil-rich salmon. The flavours here are a great balance of fresh and indulgent: salmon, grapefruit, watercress, avocado and creamy dressing. All very Californian!

1 pink grapefruit
4 x 120g salmon fillets, with skin
1 tablespoon extra-virgin olive oil
100g green beans, topped
2 large handfuls of watercress leaves
a large handful of flat-leaf parsley
a large handful of mint
1 ripe avocado, sliced

*to serve*
**green goddess dressing (right)**

Segment the grapefruit by first slicing off both ends. Stand the fruit on a board and, following its curve, slice off the peel and pith with a very sharp knife. Cut out the grapefruit segments by slicing between the membranes.

Heat a frying pan over medium–high heat for 2 minutes. Brush the salmon with oil and season well. Cook the salmon, skin-down, for 3 minutes, then turn over and cook for 1 minute; the salmon should be quite rare and the skin crispy. Remove from the pan and leave to rest for 2 minutes.

Meanwhile, blanch the beans in a pan of lightly salted boiling water for 2–3 minutes until they are bright green and tender yet crisp. Rinse under cold running water and drain well.

Arrange the watercress, parsley, mint, avocado, beans and grapefruit on serving plates. Slice the salmon and place on top, drizzle with green goddess dressing and season with sea salt to serve.
**Serves 4**

## Green goddess dressing

a large handful of watercress leaves
100g yoghurt
2–3 tablespoons mayonnaise
a large handful of mixed herbs
    (such as dill, basil, mint and parsley)
2 spring onions, chopped
juice of ½ lemon

Pulse together all the ingredients in a blender or food processor, adding a little more yoghurt or some water if needed. Refrigerate until required.
**Serves 4**

# Prawn toasts

These are almost too retro, but I just couldn't resist including them, as they always disappear in seconds when friends come over for drinks. Make them a touch more contemporary by using a mixture of black and white sesame seeds as they do at London's Michelin-starred Chinese restaurant Yauatcha.

175g raw prawns, peeled and deveined
2 spring onions, finely chopped
2 garlic cloves, finely chopped
½ teaspoon grated fresh ginger
1 egg, lightly beaten
1 teaspoon cornflour
1 thin baguette or sourdough loaf
50g sesame seeds (white, black,
    or a mixture of both)
light-flavoured oil, such as
    sunflower, for shallow-frying

*to serve*
coriander leaves

Finely chop the prawns and mix with the spring onion, garlic, ginger, egg, cornflour and sea salt and white pepper.

Cut the bread on the diagonal into 1cm slices (cut them in half if large) and spread with the prawn mixture. Sprinkle with sesame seeds and refrigerate for at least 10 minutes before cooking.

Heat the oil in a frying pan and shallow-fry the toasts, prawn-side-down, for 1 minute. Turn over carefully and fry the other side for 1 minute. Drain on kitchen paper and serve immediately, sprinkled with coriander leaves.
**Serves 6–8 as a nibble**

# Steamed fish
# with chilli dressing

Here is the meal for those days when you've not been eating as healthily as you'd like, or you're just too tired to cook 'properly' but want something simple and clean tasting. The pure flavours of the fish and greens with this lovely peppy chilli dressing are perfect. How much more basic can dinner get?

**1 pak choy, leaves separated**
**100g green beans, topped**
**100g sugarsnap peas**
**4 x 200g firm white fish fillets**

*to serve*
**chilli dressing (right)**

If you have a steamer, arrange the vegetables on a large plate with the fish fillets on top and then put in your steamer (you may have to do this in two batches). Steam for 5–10 minutes (depending on the thickness of your fish) until the fish is just opaque and the vegetables are bright green.

If you don't have a steamer, preheat your oven to 180°C/gas mark 4 and arrange the vegetables on a double piece of foil with the fish on top. Wrap the foil into a parcel and bake in the oven for 5–10 minutes (depending on the thickness of your fish) until the fish is just opaque and the vegetables are bright green.

Either way, serve the fish and vegetables immediately with the chilli dressing.
**Serves 4**

## Chilli dressing

60ml soy sauce
1 teaspoon balsamic vinegar
3 teaspoons caster sugar
1 teaspoon sesame oil
1 long red chilli, finely chopped
3 spring onions,
    finely sliced on the diagonal
1 tablespoon lime juice
1 tablespoon light-flavoured
    oil, such as sunflower

Whisk together all the ingredients and pour over the cooked fish.
**Serves 4**

# Salt and pepper squid

Many people claim this as their favourite Asian classic. They also assume it's something that can be made only by professional chefs in a restaurant. In fact, this is one of the easiest basic recipes you can make. The trick is a light batter and keeping the squid tender by cooking quickly at a very high temperature. Fish and prawns can also be cooked by the same method.

180g cornflour
170ml soda water
1 teaspoon sea salt
1 teaspoon ground
    black pepper
light-flavoured oil, such as
    sunflower, for frying
500g squid, cleaned, cut into
    6cm pieces and scored in
    a crisscross pattern
1 red chilli, finely sliced

*to serve*
lime wedges

Mix together 120g of the cornflour and the soda water to make a batter.

Season the remaining cornflour with the salt and pepper. Place a wok over medium–high heat. Heat 5cm oil in the wok until very hot.

Dust the squid in the seasoned cornflour and then dip in the batter. Fry in small batches until golden and crisp. Add the chilli for the last few seconds. Drain on kitchen paper and serve the squid with lime wedges, fried red chilli and lots more sea salt and ground black pepper.

**Serves 4**

# Fish and chips

Whether you're sitting on Bondi Beach or eating at the best restaurant in town, fish and chips has become an acceptable part of modern foodie culture. I'm not a fan of the steamed sogginess it takes on when battered and wrapped in traditional paper; I prefer these crisp, breaded goujons that can be served with home-made chips for dinner or in little baskets with drinks.

**75g plain flour**
**½ teaspoon paprika**
**1 teaspoon ground cumin**
**2 eggs, lightly beaten**
**80g fresh breadcrumbs**
**500g firm white fish fillets,**
   **cut into fat strips**
**2 tablespoons olive oil,**
   **plus extra just in case**
**25g butter, plus extra just in case**

*to serve*
**oven-baked chips (right)**
**tartare sauce (right)**
**lemon wedges**
**chopped flat-leaf parsley**

Mix the flour, paprika and cumin with sea salt and ground black pepper in a bowl. Put the eggs in another bowl. Season the breadcrumbs well with sea salt and black pepper and put in a third bowl. Dip each piece of fish in the flour, then in the egg, then in the breadcrumbs.

Heat the olive oil and butter in a large non-stick frying pan over medium–high heat. Cook the fish strips, in batches, for about 2 minutes on each side until lightly golden, adding a little more oil and butter to the pan if needed. Serve with oven-baked chips, tartare sauce, lemon wedges and a scattering of parsley.
**Serves 4**

## Oven-baked chips

1.25kg potatoes, scrubbed
   but not peeled
3 teaspoons olive oil

Preheat the oven to 230°C/gas mark 8 and put a couple of baking trays in the oven for 20 minutes to heat up. Cut the potatoes into chips, dry with a clean tea towel, toss with the oil and sprinkle with sea salt.

Put the chips on baking paper on top of the hot baking trays and bake for 30 minutes, turning once, or until golden.
**Serves 4**

## Tartare sauce

4 tablespoons mayonnaise
2 gherkins, finely chopped
2 teaspoons tiny salted capers,
   rinsed and chopped
1 tablespoon chopped flat-leaf parsley
1 teaspoon snipped chives
lemon juice, to taste

Stir together all the ingredients.
**Serves 4**

My mother is a vegetarian and so was my wife until I met her… Now I'm waiting for one of my daughters to declare she's never going to eat meat again. Actually, I wouldn't mind at all. Vegetables absolutely lead my cooking and I always feel they make the table come alive. The diversity and colours of the vegetables we can buy never ceases to excite me.

When I was younger, vegetarians had to survive on an endless diet of nut roasts and faux burgers that tasted like cardboard. I don't see any reason why that should be acceptable. I also know how disappointing it is to have to make do with chips and a side salad when you go out to eat. Or to be rather grudgingly catered for when you've been invited for dinner at a friend's (and they've forgotten about your 'fussy' food habits).

So, I've spent many years perfecting a chickpea burger that's crunchy on the outside and meltingly soft in the middle, and an elegant lasagne layered with milky ricotta and served with home-made pesto. These are basic recipes that will make anyone, meat-eater or veggie, love you forever.

# Vegetables

# Dips

What did we do before dips? It feels as if they were suddenly invented in the late seventies, spookily around the time those multi-compartment dip dishes appeared. Some people have been put off by cheap, shop-bought dips in suspect flavours, but a home-made smoky baba ganoush or lemony hummus is very very different from those too-smooth, processed varieties. Serve with toasted flatbreads or your favourite 'dipper'.

## Baba ganoush

2 aubergines (about 750g)
2 tablespoons extra-virgin olive oil
1 tablespoon tahini
2 garlic cloves, crushed
1½ tablespoons lemon juice

*to serve*
40g walnuts, lightly toasted, chopped
3 spring onions, finely chopped
chopped coriander
pomegranate seeds
extra-virgin olive oil
toasted flatbreads (page 129)

Preheat the oven to 200°C/gas mark 6 and preheat a barbecue chargrill plate. Put the aubergines directly onto the very hot chargrill and roast, turning occasionally, for 10–15 minutes until the skin is charred.

Transfer the aubergines to a baking tray and roast in the oven for a further 20 minutes, or until the flesh is soft. Leave to cool.

Once the aubergines are cool, peel off the skin and put the flesh in a food processor with the olive oil, tahini, garlic and lemon juice. Pulse until combined but still with some texture. Season with sea salt and ground black pepper.

Spoon into a serving dish, top with the walnuts, spring onion, coriander and pomegranate seeds and drizzle with a little extra-virgin olive oil. Serve with flatbreads.
Serves 4

## Hummus

Drain and rinse a 440g tin of chickpeas and put in a blender with 1 garlic clove, ½ teaspoon ground cumin, 2 tablespoons chopped coriander, 2 tablespoons lemon juice, 2 tablespoons extra-virgin olive oil, 2 tablespoons tahini and 80ml warm water. Mix until smooth. Drizzle with a little extra-virgin olive oil and sprinkle with chilli flakes to serve.
Serves 4

## Beetroot dip

Mix 450g chopped cooked beetroot, 250g Greek yoghurt, 2 tablespoons lemon juice, 1 teaspoon ground cumin and 1 teaspoon ground coriander in a blender until smooth. Season with sea salt and ground black pepper.
Serves 4

## Caramelised onion dip

Heat 2 tablespoons olive oil in a large frying pan over medium–low heat. Stir in 2 halved and thinly sliced onions and 1 teaspoon balsamic vinegar and season well. Cook for 5 minutes. Turn down the heat and cook for 35–40 minutes, or until the onion is soft and golden brown. Leave to cool.

Beat 100g cream cheese and 250g soured cream until smooth. Stir in the cooked onions with all their pan juices and serve.
Serves 4

# Chickpea burgers

Even the most committed carnivore and 'proper burger' aficionado can sometimes get a craving for a veggie burger. I speak from experience! This one has a lovely falafel-like texture: crunchy outside but nutty and wholesome within. This is real weekend fare that brings back memories of wandering around open-air markets or sitting on blankets at music festivals. I still love the burgers, but my wife has given away my poncho.

800g tinned chickpeas, drained,
   or soaked and cooked
   dried chickpeas
3 eggs
1 teaspoon sea salt
a handful of chopped coriander
a handful of chopped flat-leaf parsley
3 spring onions, finely chopped
2 teaspoons lemon zest
1 red chilli, finely chopped
   (deseeded first, if you like)
120g wholemeal breadcrumbs
3 tablespoons extra-virgin olive oil

*to serve*
6 wholemeal buns
labna or Greek yoghurt
lettuce leaves
flat-leaf parsley
finely sliced red onion
tomato slices
chilli sauce

Put the chickpeas, eggs, salt and a grind of black pepper in a food processor and blitz until nearly smooth. Transfer to a large bowl and add the coriander, parsley, spring onion, lemon zest, chilli and breadcrumbs. Stir together and leave for 5–10 minutes.

Moisten your hands with water and shape the mixture into 6 patties.

Heat the oil in a large frying pan over medium–high heat. Cook the burgers in batches for 3–4 minutes on each side until browned.

Serve the burgers in buns spread with labna or yoghurt, with lettuce, parsley, red onion, tomato and some chilli sauce.

**Serves 6**

# Roasted butternut squash, lentil and spice pasties with yoghurt dressing

My pasties are inspired more by the Middle East than by Cornwall, with turmeric in the pastry to give them that lovely golden colour, and nicely spiced lentils and butternut squash for the filling. The joke in our family is that when my mother was younger, a boyfriend gave her a necklace inscribed: 'I love you Pasty'. Her name is Patsy.

*pastry*
**300g plain flour**
**1 teaspoon turmeric**
**1 teaspoon salt**
**60ml olive oil**
**1 egg yolk**

*filling*
**800g butternut squash, peeled
and cut into 2cm cubes**
**2 tablespoons olive oil**
**1 onion, finely chopped**
**2 garlic cloves, crushed**
**1 teaspoon grated fresh ginger**
**1 teaspoon ground cinnamon**
**400g tin lentils, rinsed and drained**
**2 egg yolks, lightly beaten, to brush**

*to serve*
**yoghurt dressing (right)**
**paprika or sumac, to sprinkle**
**olive oil, to drizzle**

To make the pastry, put the flour, turmeric and salt into a large bowl. Add the oil, egg yolk and 125ml iced water. Mix with a fork until the dough comes together. Gather the dough together and transfer to a lightly floured surface. Knead until smooth and elastic. Divide into 12 balls, cover with a damp cloth and leave to rest for 1 hour.

Meanwhile, to make the filling, preheat the oven to 200°C/gas mark 6. Put the squash on a large baking tray, drizzle with 1 tablespoon of the oil and season with sea salt and black pepper. Roast in the oven for 30 minutes, or until golden.

Heat the other tablespoon of olive oil in a large frying pan over medium–high heat. Add the onion and cook, stirring occasionally, for 5 minutes until softened. Add the garlic, ginger and cinnamon and cook, stirring, for 2 minutes. Transfer to a large mixing bowl and add the lentils and roasted squash. Roughly mash with a fork and season to taste. Leave to cool.

On a lightly floured surface roll out each ball of pastry dough into a 10cm circle. Spread 2–3 tablespoons of filling over one half of each circle. Brush around the edge with water and fold the pastry over to enclose the filling and make a semicircle. Press the pastry edges together with a fork.

Put the pasties on a baking tray, brush with egg yolk and bake for 25 minutes, or until crisp and golden. Serve with yoghurt dressing, sprinkled with paprika or sumac and drizzled with a little extra oil.
**Serves 6**

## Yoghurt dressing

250g Greek yoghurt
1½ tablespoons extra-virgin olive oil
2 tablespoons lemon juice

Stir together all the ingredients and season to taste with sea salt and black pepper.
**Serves 6**

# Palak paneer

Indians are the grand masters of rich, satisfying vegetarian food. I actually stopped eating meat when I was in India, the choice of veggie dishes was so vast and so delectable. (The goats' heads lying on the side of the road might have had something to do with it, too.) This combination of delicately spiced, iron-rich spinach and paneer is great with warm naan bread, or as a side dish with grilled meat. If you don't have paneer, you can make this with firm tofu.

1 tablespoon light-flavoured
   oil, such as sunflower
1 teaspoon cumin seeds
1 onion, finely chopped
5cm piece of fresh ginger,
   peeled and grated
2 garlic cloves, crushed
2 green chillies, finely chopped
   (deseeded first, if you like)
800g spinach, thoroughly washed
   and roughly chopped
1 tablespoon ground coriander
¾ teaspoon garam masala
200g paneer, cut into small blocks
150ml single cream
20g butter
lemon juice, to taste

*to serve*
naan bread, steamed rice or
   toasted flatbreads (page 129)

Heat the oil in a large heavy-based pan over medium–low heat. Add the cumin seeds and cook for 1 minute. Add the onion and cook for 5 minutes, or until soft. Add the ginger, garlic and chilli and fry for 30 seconds.

Turn the heat to low and add the spinach and 250ml water. Cook for 8–10 minutes, then add the coriander and garam masala. Cool slightly, then purée. Return to the pan, add the paneer and season with sea salt. Add the cream and cook for 5 minutes. Stir in the butter and finish off with a squeeze of lemon juice. Serve with naan bread, rice or flatbreads.

**Serves 4**

# Green sides

You can always judge a good restaurant, I think, by the imagination and execution of its side dishes. It's great to have a few tricks up your sleeve at home, too. Anyone can boil a carrot, but how about broccolini spiked with red chilli, or green beans with salty pancetta and sautéed garlic? These can make a world of difference to a simple main course.

## Beans with garlic and pancetta

400g green beans, topped
1 teaspoon extra-virgin olive oil
1 teaspoon butter
3 garlic cloves, sliced
50g pancetta, thinly sliced

Blanch the beans in a large pan of lightly salted boiling water for 2–3 minutes until bright green and tender yet crisp. Refresh under cold running water and drain well.

Heat the olive oil and butter in a large frying pan over medium–high heat. Add the garlic and pancetta and cook, stirring, for 2 minutes until the pancetta is crisp. Add the beans and toss for 1–2 minutes to heat through. Season with sea salt and pepper.
**Serves 4**

## Broccolini with chilli

2 tablespoons olive oil
1 red chilli, deseeded and chopped
3 garlic cloves, finely chopped
2 bunches of broccolini, trimmed
lemon juice, to taste

Heat the oil in a large frying pan until very hot. Add the chilli and garlic and cook for 1 minute. Add the broccolini and enough water to cover the bottom of the pan. Cover and steam for 3–5 minutes until tender.

Remove the broccolini from the pan and simmer the pan liquid until reduced by half. Pour over the broccolini. Finish with a squeeze of lemon juice and season with sea salt and black pepper.
**Serves 4**

## Chard with olive oil and lemon

800g chard leaves, thoroughly
    washed and trimmed
2 tablespoons extra-virgin olive oil
1 tablespoon lemon juice
1 garlic clove, crushed
Parmesan shavings

Strip the chard leaves from the stalks and chop the stalks. Blanch the stalks in lightly salted boiling water for 4 minutes. Add the leaves for the last minute of cooking time. Drain and place in a bowl. Mix together the oil, lemon juice and garlic and season with sea salt and ground black pepper. Drizzle over the chard. Top with Parmesan shavings.
**Serves 4**

# Double-baked soufflés with goat's cheese and leek

Watching a soufflé rise brings out the eight-year-old wannabe scientist in me. These are great for beginners because they are so forgiving. They're quite unlike those traditional, temperamental soufflés that threaten to collapse if you so much as open the oven door to check on them. With these, you can actually let them collapse after cooking, then bake them again until puffed and golden. They make the perfect starter for a dinner party.

60g butter, plus extra for greasing
1 large leek, white part only,
    finely chopped
60g plain flour
325ml warm milk
4 eggs, separated
100g goat's cheese, crumbled
about 250ml double cream
grated Parmesan

Preheat the oven to 180°C/gas mark 4 and lightly grease four 250ml ramekins with butter. Heat the butter in a pan over medium–low heat and cook the leek for 3–5 minutes until soft and translucent. Stir in the flour and cook for 1–2 minutes until golden. Slowly whisk in the milk and simmer, stirring, until thick. Leave to cool.

Stir in the egg yolks and season with sea salt and ground black pepper. Gently stir in the goat's cheese. Beat the egg whites into firm peaks and then gradually fold into the soufflé mixture. Spoon into the ramekins.

Sit the ramekins in a roasting tin and pour water into the tin until it reaches halfway up the ramekins (this makes a bain-marie so that the soufflés cook gently). Bake in the oven for 15–20 minutes until puffed and golden. Remove the ramekins from the roasting tin and leave the soufflés to rest until cool.

Carefully turn out the soufflés into small gratin dishes (or other small ovenproof dishes). Pour a little cream over each soufflé so there is about 5mm cream in each dish. Sprinkle with Parmesan and return the soufflés to the oven for 10–12 minutes.

**Serves 4**

# Black bean chilli

There seems to be a mass Mexican wave happening at the moment, particularly in London restaurants, so black beans are everywhere. This is a contemporary version of a favourite party food that seems almost biblical in its ability to feed crowds of people. It can be stretched out even further with tortillas or rice, corn salsa and a good pile of freshly chopped coriander. This also works well with chickpeas in place of black beans.

400g black beans, rinsed and drained
    (or 800g tinned black beans)
2 tablespoons olive oil
1 onion, finely chopped
2 courgettes, chopped
2 celery stalks, finely chopped
2 garlic cloves, crushed
1 long red chilli, finely chopped
    (deseeded first, if you like)
1 teaspoon ground coriander
1 teaspoon ground cumin
4 tomatoes, chopped
juice of 1 lime

*to serve*
corn salsa (right)
crumbled feta or soured cream
avocado, diced
fresh coriander
lime wedges
warm tortillas or rice

Soak the beans for 8 hours in a bowl of cold water and then drain. Put the beans in a large saucepan and cover with water. Bring to the boil, reduce the heat and simmer for 30 minutes, then drain.

Heat the oil in a large heavy-based pan over medium–low heat. Add the onion, courgettes and celery and cook for 6–7 minutes, stirring occasionally, until slightly softened. Add the garlic, chilli and spices and cook, stirring, for 1–2 minutes until fragrant.

Stir in the tomatoes, beans and 125ml water and bring to the boil. Reduce the heat to very low and simmer, stirring frequently, for 10–15 minutes until thick. Stir in the lime juice and season with sea salt and ground black pepper.

Serve with corn salsa, feta, avocado, coriander, lime wedges and warm tortillas or rice.
Serves 4–6

## Corn salsa

1½ tablespoons olive oil
300g corn kernels,
    cut from the cob
1 small onion, finely chopped
1 tablespoon lime juice
1 green chilli, finely chopped
    (deseeded first, if you like)

Heat 1 tablespoon of the oil in a large frying pan over high heat. Add the corn and cook, stirring frequently, for 3–4 minutes. Tip the corn into a large bowl and stir in the onion, lime juice, chilli and remaining oil. Season with sea salt and pepper.
Serves 4–6

# Stir-fried tofu with chilli and basil

Tofu is one of those love-hate ingredients: people think they hate it, but then they actually try it and discover they love it. I love it because you can keep it in the fridge for weeks, forget all about it, and there it is when you want to rustle together a quick meal. Throw this into a stir-fry and the basil and chilli give it all the flavour it needs.

4 garlic cloves, crushed
1 large red chilli, chopped
    (deseeded first, if you like)
2 tablespoons light-flavoured
    oil, such as sunflower
250g tofu, cut into bite-size pieces
1 green pepper, chopped
300g asparagus, chopped
50g cashew nuts, chopped
2 tablespoons fish sauce
1 tablespoon dark soy sauce
1 tablespoon caster sugar
a small handful of basil leaves

*to serve*
steamed rice

Pound the garlic and chilli and a good pinch of sea salt with a mortar and pestle to make a paste.

Heat a wok over high heat for 1 minute. Add the oil and, when hot, add the chilli paste. Stir-fry for 15 seconds until lightly golden. Add the tofu and stir-fry until golden, then add the pepper, asparagus and cashew nuts and stir-fry for about 5 minutes until the vegetables are just cooked.

Add the fish sauce, soy sauce and sugar and stir-fry for 30 seconds. Remove from the heat and stir in the basil. Serve immediately with steamed rice.

**Serves 2**

# Lasagne

When you want a hit of veggie goodness, you don't necessarily need layers of grilled vegetables in your lasagne. The comforting quality of pure milky ricotta, combined with the simple sweetness of tomato and basil pesto, is all that's required.

**2–3 tablespoons olive oil**
**1 onion, chopped**
**2 garlic cloves, crushed**
**1.2kg tinned chopped tomatoes**
**a pinch of caster sugar**
**375g fresh lasagne or 275g dry**
   **precooked lasagne sheets**
**750g ricotta**
**250g mozzarella cheese, sliced**
**pesto (right)**
**25g grated Parmesan**

Heat half the oil in a heavy-based pan over medium heat and add the onion. Cook, stirring, for 2 minutes until softened and then add the garlic. Add the tomatoes, the remaining oil and the sugar and season with sea salt and ground black pepper. Cook over medium–low heat for a further 20 minutes until slightly reduced. Preheat the oven to 200°C/gas mark 6.

Spread a third of the tomato sauce over the base of a large ovenproof dish. Top with a layer of pasta sheets. Spread half the ricotta over the pasta and add a few slices of mozzarella. Drizzle with pesto and then top with another layer of pasta sheets. Spread with another third of the tomato sauce, the remaining ricotta and some more mozzarella. Drizzle with pesto and top with another layer of pasta sheets. Spread with the remaining tomato sauce and top with the remaining mozzarella and the Parmesan.

Cover with foil and bake for 20 minutes, then uncover and bake for 20 minutes. Serve with extra pesto to drizzle, if you like.
**Serves 6**

## Pesto

125g pine nuts
2 garlic cloves, chopped
50g grated Parmesan
a bunch of fresh basil
200ml extra-virgin olive oil
lemon juice

Whiz the pine nuts, garlic, Parmesan and basil in a food processor. With the motor running, add the olive oil, very gradually, until the pesto has a smooth consistency. Season with sea salt, ground pepper and lemon juice to taste. Pesto can be stored in a clean, airtight container for up to a week in the fridge.
**Makes 375ml**

# Baked vegetable sides

Where would we be without roast potatoes? They can melt even the hardest heart. Traditionalists will argue for parboiling and goose fat. I sometimes parboil for extra fluffiness, but goose fat doesn't have a regular place in my kitchen. I love the sweetness and colour of a medley of roasted root vegetables, perhaps with crunchy red onion tossed through. Currently my favourite vegetable is cauliflower; I like this simply roasted or finished with a dressing of olive oil, capers, lemon juice and parsley.

## Roast potatoes

600g potatoes, peeled
   and cut into quarters
3 tablespoons olive oil
1 teaspoon sea salt

Preheat the oven to 200°C/gas mark 6. Toss the potatoes in the olive oil and sea salt until evenly coated. Put the potatoes in a roasting tin and bake for 35–40 minutes, or until golden and crispy.
**Serves 4**

## Roast cauliflower

1 cauliflower, trimmed
   and cut into florets
3 tablespoons olive oil

Preheat the oven to 200°C/gas mark 6. Put the cauliflower in a roasting tin, drizzle with the olive oil, season with sea salt and black pepper and toss well to coat. Roast for 20 minutes until nicely browned.
**Serves 4**

## Roast root vegetables

4 small carrots (or larger
   carrots, chopped)
4 parsnips, sliced
4 small turnips, cut into wedges
olive oil, to drizzle
2 tablespoons red wine vinegar
1 tablespoon honey
a small handful of flat-leaf
   parsley, finely chopped
zest of 1 orange
1 garlic clove, crushed

Preheat the oven to 200°C/gas mark 6. Put all the vegetables in a large roasting tin, drizzle with the olive oil, season with sea salt and ground black pepper and toss well to coat. Roast in the oven for 45 minutes to 1 hour. Drizzle with the vinegar and honey.

Mix together the parsley, orange zest and garlic. Season with sea salt and ground black pepper and sprinkle over the roasted vegetables just before serving.
**Serves 4**

Unusually for a chef, I have a sweet tooth, which seems only to get sweeter as I get older (or perhaps that's what living in a household of four girls has done to me). As far as I'm concerned, a cheeseboard at the end of a meal will never evoke the same response as a golden tarte Tatin, hot from the oven and drowning in cream.

Food fashions certainly come and go, but some puddings remain eternally popular. If you can add them to your basic repertoire you'll raise every meal to great heights. Crème caramel is probably one of the first restaurant sweets I ever tasted. It seemed so sophisticated back then, arriving in its little pool of toffee-flavoured syrup. It's still a favourite of mine today, although I've tweaked the recipe a little for fun.

My mother's chocolate mousse cake (only ever made for dinner parties and decorated with whipped cream and mint-crisp chocolates) I thought was the most glamorous thing I'd ever seen as a small child. It's here in all its glory, although I've made a few twenty-first-century adjustments to that recipe, too. Thanks, Mum.

# Desserts

# Crêpes

Everyone needs to know how to make a crêpe. There are few things that look more flash in the kitchen than flipping a crêpe with a casual twist of the wrist. Do make sure you can catch it again, though — there are few things that look less flash in the kitchen than crêpe all over the stovetop.

150g plain flour
2 eggs, lightly beaten
250ml milk
50g unsalted butter, melted and
    cooled, plus extra for cooking

*to serve*
lemon juice
sugar

Put the flour, eggs, milk and butter in a blender with a pinch of sea salt and whiz together. Refrigerate for 1 hour.

Heat a non-stick frying pan over medium heat and brush with a little butter. Ladle 3 tablespoons of batter into the pan and tip the pan to quickly and evenly spread the batter. (If you find the mixture a bit thick, add an extra tablespoon or two of milk.) Cook for 1 minute, then lift the edge of the crêpe and flip it over. Cook for just a couple of seconds on the other side. Keep warm while you make the rest of the crêpes.

Serve folded, with a squeeze of lemon juice and a scattering of sugar.
**Makes 8**

## Double chocolate crêpes

Add 2 tablespoons cocoa powder to the batter and cook as above. Spread with chocolate hazelnut spread, fold and serve.
**Makes 8**

# Crème caramel

This was another dilemma: crème caramel or brulée? Any dish requiring a blow torch after a long working day and a few glasses of wine with dinner, doesn't seem the most sensible option to me. And crème caramel is a childhood favourite: I can't go past it, even now. I use part coconut milk (perfect for after Asian meals), but you can replace that with milk if you prefer. I like to make one big pudding rather than individual ramekins — I love cutting it into wobbly slices.

170g caster sugar
375g tin sweetened
   condensed milk
5 eggs
600ml milk
400ml tin half-fat coconut milk

Preheat the oven to 180°C/gas mark 4. To make the caramel, put the sugar in a small heavy-based pan over medium heat. Stir occasionally with a fork until the sugar has dissolved and the caramel is dark golden. Remove from the heat and pour carefully into a non-metallic 23cm ovenproof dish (hold the dish with a tea towel while you pour the hot caramel). Put the dish in a deep roasting tin.

Whisk together the condensed milk, eggs, milk and coconut milk. Strain into the dish over the caramel. Pour hot water into the roasting tin to reach halfway up the dish (this turns it into a bain-marie), cover the tin with foil and bake for 1 hour. Test if it's ready by lifting the foil and jiggling the dish — the custard will look set but wobble like a jelly. Remove the dish from the tin, cool and refrigerate for at least 4 hours.

To serve, run a small knife around the edge of the dish and then put a serving plate on top. Carefully turn both the dish and serving plate over, holding them firmly together, then lift off the dish.
**Serves 8**

# Tiramisu

Before coffee-lovers had their own machines at home, I remember going to the local coffee shop and carrying home strong espressos to make tiramisu. You can make do with instant but I like the kick from using real java and grated dark chocolate on top. They cut through the creamy sweet mascarpone and do as the name suggests in Italian: pick me up.

500ml very strong coffee
  (if you have only instant, use
  4 tablespoons coffee powder),
  at room temperature
60ml Marsala
60ml Tia Maria
3 eggs, separated
110g caster sugar
400g mascarpone
300g savoiardi biscuits
125ml lightly whipped cream
grated dark chocolate, to dust

Mix together the coffee, Marsala and Tia Maria in a shallow bowl and set aside.

Beat the egg yolks and 80g of the sugar with electric beaters until thick and pale. Beat in the mascarpone until just combined.

In a separate bowl, beat the egg whites with a pinch of sea salt until soft peaks form. Gradually add the remaining sugar and beat until stiff peaks form. Gently fold the egg whites into the mascarpone mixture with a large metal spoon.

Soak a savoiardi biscuit in the coffee for a few seconds, then lay in the base of a 2 litre serving dish. Use half the biscuits to cover the base of the dish, trimming the biscuits if necessary so they fit snugly. Spread the mascarpone mixture over the biscuits.

Make a second layer of biscuits in the same way as before. Top with the whipped cream, cover the dish with cling film and chill, preferably overnight. When ready to serve, dust with grated chocolate.

**Serves 8–10**

# Lemon tart

Lemon tart is eternally popular, partly, I think, because people see it as a 'light' dessert. Sadly, despite its demure appearance, it does contain all the usual pudding-friendly suspects. My lemon tart, however, is a little different as it comes without the pastry. So, as well as being much easier to make, it really is lighter, without skimping on my favourite part: the zesty filling.

**3 eggs**
**75g plain flour**
**230g caster sugar**
**125g unsalted butter, melted**
**zest of 2 unwaxed lemons**
**150ml lemon juice**
**300ml single cream**

*to serve*
**icing sugar**
**cream or crème fraîche**

Preheat the oven to 180°C/gas mark 4. Lightly grease a 20cm round springform tin.

Whisk the eggs and then gradually whisk in the flour. Add the caster sugar, butter, lemon zest and juice, cream and a pinch of sea salt and whisk well. Pour into the tin and bake for 40–45 minutes, until slightly browned.

Leave in the tin to cool for 20 minutes before turning out and slicing. Dust with icing sugar and serve with cream or crème fraîche.

**Serves 6–8**

# Pavlova with brown sugar and strawberries

I like my meringues to be old-fashioned and gooey in the middle, rather than bright white and explosive. The vinegar and arrowroot give this a chewy centre, and I add soft brown sugar for its caramel flavouring and gorgeous golden colour. Pavlova is traditionally a summery dessert, but this one, with its warmer colouring, also works beautifully in winter with torn figs instead of strawberries.

**6 egg whites**
**¼ teaspoon cream of tartar**
**1 teaspoon vanilla extract**
**230g caster sugar**
**80g soft brown sugar**
**1 tablespoon cornflour**
**2 tablespoons arrowroot**
**2 teaspoons white vinegar**

*to serve*
**300ml whipping cream**
**150g Greek yoghurt**
**500g strawberries,**
    **hulled and halved**
**1–2 tablespoons honey**

Preheat the oven to 200°C/gas mark 6. Draw a 20cm circle on a sheet of baking paper and place the paper on a large baking tray.

Beat the egg whites with the cream of tartar and vanilla until stiff peaks form. Add the caster sugar and brown sugar, 1 tablespoon at a time, beating until all the sugar is incorporated and dissolved and the mixture is thick and glossy. Stir in the cornflour, arrowroot and vinegar.

Pile the mixture into the circle on the paper and spread gently into shape with a spatula. Put in the oven and reduce the temperature immediately to 130°C/gas mark ½. Bake for 1 hour 20 minutes, then turn off the oven, prop the door ajar and leave the pavlova inside until completely cooled.

To serve, lightly whip the cream and yoghurt together and spread over the pavlova. Toss the strawberries in the honey and arrange over the top. Serve immediately.
**Serves 8–10**

# Banana split

The banana split is such an enduring image of happiness, bringing to mind those wonderful American diners of the 1950s. I like to lighten up the chocolate sauce with coconut milk and grill the bananas first so that they're soft and gooey.

**4 small bananas, split in half lengthways**
**40g unsalted butter, cubed**
**25g caster sugar**

*to serve*
**vanilla or coconut ice cream**
**coconut chocolate sauce (right)**
**shredded coconut**

Heat your grill to medium. Put the bananas on a baking tray, dot with the cubes of butter and sprinkle with caster sugar. Grill until caramelised.

Serve the bananas, topped with the ice cream, coconut chocolate sauce and shredded coconut.

**Serves 4**

## Coconut chocolate sauce

400ml tin coconut milk
60g light muscovado sugar
1 teaspoon vanilla extract
200g dark chocolate, chopped

Put the coconut milk, sugar and vanilla in a saucepan over medium heat and stir until the sugar dissolves. Increase the heat and bring to the boil. Remove from the heat and whisk in the chocolate until melted and smooth. Keep in the fridge in an airtight container and melt over low heat to use.

**Makes about 500ml**

# Tarte Tatin

A French name can make any dish sound rather daunting… so chic to order in a restaurant but surely a nightmare to make yourself? Tarte Tatin is actually much easier than you'd imagine, and my cheat's version simplifies it further by making the caramel with the apples already arranged in the pan. I like my tart to be really well cooked, so the caramel is toffee-like and almost burnt.

375g block puff pastry,
 thawed but very cold
60g unsalted butter, softened
110g caster sugar
6–8 green apples, peeled,
 cored and quartered

*to serve*
cream or crème fraîche

First, roll out the pastry into a 25cm-wide circle. Place on a lined tray and refrigerate.

Preheat the oven to 220°C/gas mark 7. Rub the butter over the base of a 25cm ovenproof frying pan and then sprinkle with the sugar. Pack the apple pieces, sideways on, in tight concentric circles that are as neat as you can make them. Place the pan over medium–high heat until the caramel is golden brown and bubbly. (Don't be afraid to let it really caramelise.) Remove from the heat.

Lay the pastry over the apples, tucking the edge down between the side of the pan and the apples. Bake for 20–25 minutes, or until the pastry is puffed and golden brown. Leave to stand for a few minutes and then carefully turn out onto a plate. Serve with cream or crème fraîche.

**Serves 6–8**

# Peach and blueberry pudding

Like a cobbler or a crumble, but even simpler to make, this is an unashamedly homely, country-style pudding that's great for using up any fruit going soft in the bowl. To me it feels particularly autumnal, with dark berries and stone fruit glinting through the golden batter. It's equally good made with plums and raspberries — and perfect with a cup of coffee the next morning, too.

170g caster sugar
1 teaspoon cornflour
600g peaches or nectarines,
    pitted and quartered
150g self-raising flour
1 egg
125ml milk
125g unsalted butter,
    melted and cooled
1 teaspoon vanilla extract
zest of 1 lemon
125g blueberries

*to serve*
Greek yoghurt, cream or ice cream

Preheat the oven to 180°C/gas mark 4 and lightly grease a 1 litre baking dish.

Put 3 tablespoons of the sugar in the baking dish with the cornflour and peaches and toss until the fruit is coated. Arrange evenly over the base of the dish. Bake for 15 minutes until softened.

Meanwhile, sift the flour and a pinch of sea salt into a large bowl and stir in the remaining sugar. Make a well in the centre. Whisk together the egg, milk, butter, vanilla and lemon zest and pour into the well in the dry ingredients. Stir until smooth.

When you get the peaches out of the oven, sprinkle with half the blueberries. Gently pour in the batter and scatter with the remaining blueberries.

Bake for 30–35 minutes, or until a skewer poked into the middle comes out clean. Leave to cool slightly for 5 minutes, then serve with yoghurt, cream or ice cream.
**Serves 6–8**

# Baked lemon cheesecake

I always think there's something rather wholesome and old-fashioned about baked cheesecake, in comparison to its chillier, creamier cousin. To give this an Italian twist, I sometimes use crushed almond biscotti for my base and replace the soured cream with mascarpone. Lime is also great as a tangy change from lemon.

125g plain sweet biscuits
    (digestives are best)
50g ground almonds
70g unsalted butter, melted
500g cream cheese, softened
220g caster sugar
4 eggs
1 egg yolk
grated zest and juice of
    1 large lemon
400g soured cream
1 teaspoon vanilla extract

*to serve*
icing sugar, to dust

Preheat the oven to 140°C/gas mark 1 and grease and line the base of a 24cm round springform tin. Mix the biscuits to crumbs in a food processor. Mix together the biscuit crumbs, ground almonds and melted butter and press into the bottom of the tin. Put in the fridge while you make the topping.

Mix the cream cheese and sugar in a food processor until smooth. Add the eggs, egg yolk, lemon zest and juice and mix again. Add the soured cream and vanilla extract and mix again until completely smooth.

Pour the filling over the base and bake for 1 hour (the cheesecake will still have a definite wobble in the centre). Turn the oven off and leave the cheesecake to cool inside for 1 hour. Transfer to a wire rack to cool completely before covering and refrigerating overnight. Run a knife around the inside edge of the tin to loosen the cheesecake, then lift off the side. Dust with icing sugar to serve.
**Serves 10–12**

# Chocolate mousse cake

It's funny how you grow to like dark chocolate as you get older. I only really 'got' the bittersweet attraction, along with marmalade and slippers, when I hit forty. I'm expecting to develop a taste for marzipan and macramé when I reach seventy.

150g dark chocolate, chopped
150g unsalted butter, chopped
5 eggs, separated
150g caster sugar

*chocolate mousse*
200g dark chocolate, chopped
30g unsalted butter
3 eggs, separated
300ml whipping cream, whipped

*to serve*
25g dark chocolate, finely grated

Preheat the oven to 180°C/gas mark 4. Grease and line a 24cm springform cake tin. Put the chocolate and butter in a heatproof bowl over a pan of simmering water, making sure the water isn't touching the base of the bowl. Stir until melted and smooth, then remove from the heat. Allow to cool to room temperature (so that the chocolate doesn't seize when the egg is added).

Whisk the egg whites with a pinch of sea salt in a large dry bowl until soft peaks form. Add half the sugar, 1 tablespoon at a time, whisking until the mixture is glossy and stiff.

In another bowl, beat the egg yolks with the remaining sugar until pale and increased in volume. Carefully stir into the melted chocolate and then fold gently through the egg whites with a large metal spoon. Scoop into the tin and bake for 45–50 minutes, or until a skewer poked into the centre comes out clean.

Leave the cake to cool in the tin. It will sink a little. Turn out of the tin.

For the mousse, melt the chocolate and butter in a bowl over a pan as before, and leave to cool. Whisk the egg whites in a clean dry bowl until soft peaks form. Beat the egg yolks into the cooled chocolate, one at a time. Fold in the cream and egg whites in two batches. Spread over the cooled cake and refrigerate until set. Scatter with grated dark chocolate to serve.

**Serves 10–12**

# Index

# Index

# For Natalie, Edie, Inès and Bunny

My sincere and grateful thanks to: Alison Cathie, Jane O'Shea, Helen Lewis and the team at Quadrille for their expertise and guidance in our creation of this book and for taking it on its journey into the big wide world; Rick McKenna, Greg Sitch and Davids Darzins for clarity of vision, guiding us all through the early stages of the book and making it a true reality, at all times of night and day, and through some truly tough challenges; Fran Caratti, Griff Pamment, Celeste Wilde, Tanya Freymundt, the bills' managers and head chefs, and the rest of the team at bills, who keep the vision alive day to day — you are treasured beyond measure, thank you for everything; Erika Oliveira for her enthusiasm and sheer talent and constantly paring back our vision to its very essence; Mikkel Vang for capturing beauty and spirit on film, and his energy and drive that kept us all jumping; Mary Libro for channelling me, for being unflappable and for her commitment to making it all pull together into a perfect package; Jane Price for her sense of humour, patience and leadership in the face of inexperience, on whom we relied so much, and for extracting the best from me; Summer Litchfield for chewing the fat and her sunshine and light; my army of testers — Laura, Kate, Abi, Grace, Chrissy, Emma — who tirelessly made my recipes day-in day-out, again and again, with me driving them just a little crazy; Geraldine, Chen and Meg for their impeccable taste and realising it; Marianna Cseh, Caroline Choker and Megan Morton who made our kitchen a reality with superhuman effort; Monica Hall who knew how to get us all there with supreme organisation and gentle coaxing; Emma Robertson who whipped me into shape with perpetual good humour; Jill Donald for her hand holding and generosity with her knowledge — we couldn't have done it without you; Nick and Paul for their dedicated transformation of our pictures, getting them from film to press; Mariana Sola who is a constant delight and who makes our Sydney life a joy; Patsy for her dedicated and loving support of our family; and of course to my wonderful family who makes every creative journey so much fun.

Creative Director: Erika Oliveira
Photographer: Mikkel Vang
Design: Mary Libro, Feeder
Editor: Jane Price
Merchandising: Geraldine Muñoz
Interior styling: Chen Lu assisted by Meg Jefferies
Food preparation: Julie Ballard, Grace Campbell, Peta Dent, Hamish Ingram, Kirrily La Rosa, Jacque Malouf, Griff Pamment, Abi Ulgiati
Recipe testing: Grace Campbell, Chrissy Freer, Laura Fyfe, Emma Lyttelton, Kate McCullough, Abi Ulgiati
Producer: Natalie Elliott
Production for photography: Monica Hall and Celeste Wilde
Post production: Victoria Jefferys

For Quadrille:
Publishing Director: Jane O'Shea
Creative Director: Helen Lewis
Production: Vincent Smith, Ruth Deary

The publisher, Bill Granger and the creative team would like to sincerely thank the following for their generosity and contribution to the creation of this book: Poggen Pohl Australia for the kitchen, Corian CASF for the benchtop, Miele, Helen Stephens from the divine All Hand Made for use of her home, the gallery and her exquisite ceramics, Ondene, Anibou, Bison Australia, Robert MacPherson of Yuill Crowley Gallery, Brent Harris of Kaliman Gallery, Tibet Gallery, Simon Johnson, Ici et La, Virgine Batterson and Manon et Gwanaelle, Poliform for furniture, Planet Furniture, Mud Australia, KitchenAid, Le Creuset, David Mellor, Sprouts, Sydney Fish Market, Hudson Meats, Pasta Emilia and Earth Food Store.

All spoon measures are level unless otherwise stated and 1 tablespoon equals 15ml.

Cooking temperatures and times relate to conventional ovens. If you are using a fan-assisted oven, set the oven temperature 20 degrees or 1 gas mark lower. For baking, I recommend a conventional oven rather than a fan-assisted oven.

Anyone who is pregnant or in a vulnerable health group should consult their doctor regarding eating raw or lightly-cooked eggs.

First published in 2010 by
Quadrille Publishing Limited
Alhambra House, 27–31 Charing Cross Road,
London, WC2H 0LS
www.quadrille.co.uk

Text © 2010 William Granger
Photography © 2010 Mikkel Vang
Design and layout © 2010 bills Licensing Pty Limited

Cataloguing in Publication Data: a catalogue record for this book is available from the British Library.
ISBN 978 184400 843 8
Printed in China

www.bills.com.au